T0129093

When the Running Stops

Running

Stops

My Journey
An Autobiography

Rosalind Noreiga

ARCHWAY
PUBLISHING

Archway Publishing books may be ordered through booksellers or by contacting:

Archway Publishing
1663 Liberty Drive
Bloomington, IN 47403
www.archwaypublishing.com
1 (888) 242-5904

Because of the dynamic nature of the Internet, any web addresses or links contained in this book may have changed since publication and may no longer be valid. The views expressed in this work are solely those of the author and do not necessarily reflect the views of the publisher, and the publisher hereby disclaims any responsibility for them.

Any people depicted in stock imagery provided by Getty Images are models, and such images are being used for illustrative purposes only. Certain stock imagery © Getty Images.

Scripture taken from the King James Version of the Bible.

ISBN: 978-1-4808-7365-0 (sc)
ISBN: 978-1-4808-7364-3 (e)

Library of Congress Control Number: 2018968599

Print information available on the last page.

Archway Publishing rev. date: 1/9/2019

This Light
By: Rosalind Noreiga

I heard a voice, it was the Lord's
He spoke to me, I listened
He sent me a light in the midst of my darkness
I followed that light, the light guided me
The light is so bright it warmed me
I now feel free, free from worries, free of pain
I am not afraid, I trust this light, for I know this light will lead me
to a path of peace, righteousness and prosperity
I trust this light
This light shall take me through the valleys, the hills,
and one day to the top of the mountains
I have been in the dark, I have been searching for the light
I found the light, it's here now, I embrace this light
Each day this light gets brighter
I like this light, it has brought me peace
I want to share this light with others, for this light is real
I prayed that others will see this light and believe
If you believe there is a light among the darkness
Then you must follow this light
Trust in the light and it shall warm you
You too shall feel free and emancipated
Embrace the light
For the light is real

Introduction (Prologue)

My Story: This thing called Life

Life is nothing but a journey. None of us ask to enter this journey but I believe each and every one of us were placed here by God for a specific purpose. For some, the journey may be short, and the roads traveled on may be smooth and completely paved. For others, it may be long on sometimes paved, dirt, or gravel roads with many turns, humps, and bumps along the way. No one knows how long the ride will be, but we all know is that one day the journey will end. No one knows when or how we will reach our destination. The beauty of this thing called life is that we are not in it alone. Throughout the journey, we will pick up passengers who will travel with us to help us navigate. Some of these passengers are temporarily placed in our lives by God to serve a specific purpose at a specific time and move on. Others however, are placed permanently to travel with us through the end.

Along the way, some of us find our purpose in life and serve it well. For others, it is a struggle. When it will end is not as important as to what we make of it, how we live it, the choices we make, and how we treat people along the way. What you make of it may bring you success or failure. However with each experience, good or bad, there is a lesson to be learned, and to grow from. We may at times view the challenge as obstacles or setbacks, but it often turns out to be a set up by God for greater things to come in your life.

Life can be filled with surprises. Despite the bumps, bruises, adversities, changes, and obstacles we may at times encounter, we must keep the faith in God, ourselves, and our abilities. These challenges are often God's way of bringing us closer to him, encouraging spiritual growth. Having faith gives us hope, and hope produces patience. From these life experiences, one will find courage, strength, and endurance. The key to this journey is the ability to persevere, to never give up, and to embrace both the good and the bad. Live in and enjoy the present. Although the future is not promised, we should not look back, but keep looking forward.

My journey in this precious life began fifty six years ago. Blessed to be born and raised from great parents with great parenting skills. I learned from them through their teaching that life is not always a bed of roses, and that it comes with many highs and lows. It is not about what life gives you, but what you take from it, and what you make of it will determine your success or failure. On this journey, the ride began on a very rough dirt road. This road, at times, was winding with some sharp curves and steep hills to climb. I fell off the road several times but found the courage and strength to pick myself up and continue the journey. Gradually, the road became graveled and then one day, after a miracle from God gifted me with a second chance of life, I began to see paved roads, and the ride became smoother. I know tomorrow is not promised to me, but now I approach life like I am running a marathon. I pace myself, building endurance, enjoying myself so when the finish line is near, I will have no regrets but to celebrate the journey traveled.

In order to navigate through life well, it helps that the foundation given in early childhood by your parents be a solid one. Mine was built with instillation of discipline, great values of life, love, family, hard work, togetherness, and God. Courage, bravery, determination, strength, and endurance were exemplified daily by my parents. These values became very instrumental for me in navigating through the challenges, bumps, and bruises that I faced throughout the years. Although a rough ride, I did not give up and will not give up. Instead, I kept pursuing. Through each challenge or event I persist and keep persisting until it gets better. I work harder, set goals, kept the faith. Keeping the faith was the key. Faith in God and in my abilities brought me through with a smile. This faith gives me hope and with hope the challenges became easier to deal with. My resources, (the passengers) that God has placed in my life to make the journey easier, I call upon each and every one of them, when needed, to help me through the challenges.

I am not afraid of the journey because I acknowledge that I am not in it alone. It is never lonely, how can it be when the driver of this journey, the Holy Spirit, is always with me. I strongly believe that God does not give you more than you can handle. Which means that if I get a heavier load to carry then my neighbor does, I will take it as a compliment from God. He knows my strength and weaknesses and if he chose to give me a heavy load, I must be stronger than I give myself credit for. My mother taught me to do well towards others and to give unconditionally. She taught me to live a good life and the karma will be returned to you one day. So I did, and still do, and boy was she right. It has returned abundantly to me, just when I needed it.

I was taught to be independent, work hard for what you want, and what you believe in. I did just that with so much focus on achieving mostly materialistic things. Taking care of everyone else, and at times forgetting to take care of me. I worked hard, so many hours at times even when I was sick, cashing that money to obtain worldly things that we craved for and neglecting to take the time to enjoy the simple things that God created which surrounds us: the beauty of life like the birds, the bees, the beaches. I was not taking time to enjoy the sunrise, sunset, or to smell the roses, but instead taking all the beauty that surrounds me for granted. Not realizing that it can be gone in the blink of an eye. Then one day, darkness overcame me and I thought that it was the end. It hit with such a force that I certainly felt that it would be the last breath I'd take. I was totally unprepared, but who is every truly prepared for death? But God had other plans for me. Although I came so close to death, he was there with me and saved me. It was not my time, but it sure was a wakeup call for me. Now I am re-examining my priorities and my purpose in this life, and living it to the fullest. I recognize that tomorrow is not promised, this time taking as much time I need to smell the roses, enjoy natures beauty, and spend more time with what matters most, the people in my life. This is now my second life and I intend to enjoy every minute of each day.

Contents

That Faithful Day
In the midst of darkness there was a light
That light brought me hope
Through that hope my faith deepens
From that faith I drew strength
Through that strength I found courage
That courage allowed me to endure and persevere

Chapter 1

That Faithful Day

Tuesday May 23, 2016, began like an ordinary day at my home in Lanham Maryland. The sky was bright and blue and the sun was beaming in all its glory. I was off work, and it was my gym day. But, of course, being a single mother, I had tons of other things to do that day. I had to run some errands, tidy the house and so on. *I would do those things first then go to the gym,* I told myself. I accomplished all tasks, and now it was 5:30 pm. There was now time to go to the gym, but it was raining. What the hell! That had never stopped me before. I was still going to the gym. I got dressed, got my iPod and gym bag, and was ready to go. But wait, this diva couldn't leave the house until she checked herself in the mirror to make sure she looked divine, because you never know who or what you may run into on the way. Perhaps Mr. Right or Mr. Right Now, who knows? So I went to check myself in the mirror. *Yes, I am looking good,* I said to myself, but then the strangest thing happened. A voice said, "You are not going to the gym today." Sometimes you hear a voice, call it intuition or whatever it is. I knew from personal experience that when I heard this voice but went against it, I would tend to regret it later when something bad happened.

Today however, it was more than just the voice. When I looked in the mirror, my lips were moving, but I was not speaking. At first I thought it was weird and turned to go, but the voice became stronger, "No gym today, no gym today!" It was like someone else was in the room echoing these words but I was home alone. It was so strange, however, that got the better of me and I decided okay, I wouldn't go to the gym today. Instead I'd do my workout routine downstairs in the guestroom as I sometimes did.

My workout routine that day began with twenty-five jumping jacks to warm-up, followed by twenty squats and twenty four front lunges, and finally twenty five push-ups. I was doing my routine feeling fine, pumped, no headache, nothing. After completing the twenty-five push-ups during my last routine, I stood up but felt very dizzy. Then the room felt as though it were spinning. Then, bam, bam! My head. I felt as though someone had smashed my head in two with a brick. Suddenly, the room went pitch black for a minute or two.

I stood frozen in my space, unable to move, not sure what just happened. I believe I went in and out of consciousness. Then I saw a glimmer of light. I could hear myself saying something was wrong. Oh boy! I was home alone and the phone was upstairs. *I have to get upstairs,* I kept saying.

Then the voice returned and lead me to the sofa, not far from where I was exercising. I lay on the couch for a period of time; I was not sure how long I lay there. Before I woke up, I saw a very bright light. It was so bright. Then I stood up and as I did so I felt somewhat better. My head did not hurt as much, and I found the strength to go up the stairs. I had ten steps to climb: the first five, then a platform where the front door was located. When I got to the platform I unlocked the door sensing that I would most definitely need help and if I was unconscious when help arrived, then they could not enter without breaking down the doors. Then I climbed the other five stairs that took me to the second level and to my bedroom. My phone was laying on the nightstand next to my bed and so was my blood pressure machine. The first thing I did after laying on my bed was take my blood pressure. It read 198/113. *Wow!* I thought, *This was never my BP.* Something was definitely wrong.

At this time I was employed at Washington Adventist Hospital in Maryland, about thirty minutes from my home. Earlier that day I had spoken to my nurse colleagues and friend Michelle who worked the day shift with me. Michelle lived about ten minutes from my house and passed in front of my cross street from the main road to go to work. Michelle had told me that today she would be working the evening shift. My first thought was to call Michelle and ask her to stop by my house on her way to work. So I did and fortunately for me she answered her phone even though she was driving and her ringer was on vibrate at the time.

"Michelle could you pass by my house on your way to work? I think something is wrong with me," I said.

"Okay, Roz. I am three minutes away; I will be there," she said.

I also worked with Jennifer, another nurse colleague, who lived about five minutes from my house. Jennifer worked the day shift at another hospital and would also be home at that time. I called Jennifer, unaware of whether I had dialed her mobile or home phone. Jennifer had a history of not answering her home phone, but later I learned that was the number I dialed. Fortunately, she picked up. I said the same thing to her, telling her I thought something was wrong with me.

Next, I called my son, Kyle, who was at work about a one hour drive away.

"Kyle you need to come home; something is wrong with me," I said. "It's raining; please drive carefully and take your time. I have Jen and Michelle on their way."

Now it was time to inform Robert. Robert is my dearest, special friend, and significant other but he lived in Virginia. I phoned him and fortunately he too answered by the second ring. I repeated my story to him. He is a retired firefighter, emergency medical technician (EMT, First Responder). I did not think I was panicking but he could tell from my breathing that something was wrong and he went straight into EMT mode.

"Roz you have to slow your breathing, you are going into a panic breathe with me Roz," he said. "You need to bring your blood pressure down, and this is going to do it until the paramedics get there."

Now I knew I had to call 911, but something was telling me I had to wait for Jennifer. It seemed I was not in full control, but someone more powerful than any of us was in control. In retrospect, I can now certainly say the Holy Spirit was in my room the entire time.

While on the phone with Robert, there was a loud bang on the door. It was Michelle. I yelled that it was open and to come in, but she did not hear me. I called her phone but she did not take her phone to the door, so I had no choice but to get out of bed to open the door for her.

"Rob, Michelle is at the door. I have to go open it," I said.

"Ok but get up and walk slowly, I will stay on the phone with you," said Rob.

I got down the stairs, opened the door, let Michelle in, and walked back up the stairs to my bed without feeling dizzy. Michelle stayed with me, continued to monitor my blood pressure and breathing until Jennifer came. When Jennifer came a few minutes later, Michelle left for work. Jennifer took my blood pressure another time, while Rob was still holding on the phone. This time my blood pressure was 200/115, and it was time to call 911.

"Rob, hang up we are calling 911," I said.

"Okay, I will check with Kyle to see which hospital they take you to, and I will be there," he said.

When Jennifer and I were working together at Prince Georges Hospital Center, on the Med-Surgical floor, we were always the first two nurses in the room when a code or rapid response was called.

"Well Jen it looks like we're conducting our own rapid response, only this time I am the patient, and the intensivist in my room is God," I said.

Jen called 911 and within five minutes the paramedics were at my door.

"Please take me to Washington Adventist Hospital. That's where my cardiologist practices, and where I work," I remembered saying to the paramedics.

I was thinking it was my heart, as I had problems with my heart in the past though never could have imagined what I discovered later. The paramedics told me they had to follow protocol and take me to the hospital closest to my home which was Doctor's Community Hospital. Jennifer rode with me in the ambulance and later I realized why Jennifer was called and I had to wait for her. I believed this was part of God's plan.

As the ambulance was about to pull off, my son arrived. He followed the ambulance to the hospital. I do not remember anything that happened after being placed into the ambulance nor what took place at Doctor's Community Hospital. I must have slipped into unconsciousness again.

I later learned that Jennifer was my spokesperson and advocate during the time spent in Doctor's Hospital emergency room. As a result I was treated with speed and priority. What I do remember after opening my eyes again was seeing a young man of Filipino decent with a well-built body, very muscular, wearing a helmet and a stethoscope around his neck. I did not know where I was, and I was thinking this guy is cute.

Look at those guns he looks good, I thought, referring to his biceps and triceps. Then I asked him where I was, and he told me he was my flight nurse. They had to medivac me to Washington Hospital Center due to an emergency I suffered. God must have a sense of humor because I do not remember anything after leaving my home, and not much during or after recovery but I distinctly remembered this guy.

Chapter 2

That Faithful Day part 2

They took me to the emergency room at Washington Hospital Center, and I must have blacked out again. The next time I opened my eyes, there was a male Asian doctor and a female doctor standing over me. I was attempting to get out of the stretcher, unsure of what was happening.

"I have to go to work, I have to call them, what time is it? I am going to be late for work, please let me go," I kept repeating.

"You can't go to work today. What's your work number? I will call and let them know," the Asian doctor said. Somehow, I remembered my work number and gave it to him as he called and informed them. That must have calmed me down, somewhat. When he returned, he broke down to me exactly what was happening.

"My name is Dr. Lieu, and this is Dr. Gluck the anesthesiologist. You had an accident at home, and from your friend Jennifer's account you passed out during exercising," He told me. "They took you to Doctors Community Hospital where they took a CT scan of your head and found a ruptured brain aneurysm, which means you are bleeding around your brain. They could not treat you there, so they called us, and we had to medivac you to this hospital. You are now at Washington

Hospital Center in DC, it was an emergency so we have to take you to the operating room now. If you cannot sign consent forms who can sign for you?"

"My son," I said.

"This is what we are going to do. We will attempt to coil the aneurysm to stop the bleeding, and if we are unable to do this we will have to open up your head and attempt a craniotomy to clip it. This is what could happen, you could have a seizure, stroke, or you could die," Dr. Lieu said.

Upon hearing these three words: seizure, stroke, or death, my body froze. I was numb, silent, and I did not cry. I did not ask, why me God? I did not fuss with the doctors, despite being known to. I have always lived a healthy lifestyle through mind, body, and spirit so of course I wanted to fuss, but today I just surrendered myself to God and the neurosurgical team of doctors and nurses he had chosen to care for me. And so, they rolled me into the operating room for surgery.

I was not sure how long it took, nor what time or day it was, but when I did open my eyes some time later, there was the same doctor, Dr. Lieu, looking at me.

"I am alive," I said to him.

"Yes you are, and this is what we did. We were able to successfully coil the aneurysm, but we found a second one. This one is intact, located in the middle of the right side of your head. It is fairly small in size at this time. We will not worry about that one now, we will take care of that later. We will keep you in the ICU for at least two weeks to monitor you closely because after having this type of procedure, complications are highly likely. You can still have a stroke, a seizure or swelling in your brain. We will treat you with preventive medication for these," He said.

Dr. Lieu was the neuroradiologist. He worked closely with Dr.

Rocco Armonda, the neurosurgeon, and Dr. Aulisi, the neurologist. What a great neurology team I had on my side working on me.

An aneurysm occurs when a part of a blood vessel becomes weak and fills with blood, causing the vessel to balloon or bulge. This often resembles a berry on a stick. Aneurysms can occur in any blood vessel in the body. However, brain aneurysms are the most life-threatening. When it becomes weakened it can rupture and bleed into the brain. As mine was not detected before it ruptured, the best option of treatment, per the Neurosurgeon, was coiling, also known as Endovascular Coil Embolization.

"This is a minimally invasive procedure during which a small incision is made in the groin, and small tubes and wires are navigated through the blood vessels to the aneurysm in the brain. Tiny, soft metal coils, are then pushed through the tube and placed into the aneurysm. These coils compact to create a tiny metal ball that helps prevent blood flow from entering the aneurysm, thereby relieving the pressure pushing against the walls of the aneurysm," Dr. Lieu said.

So much was said to me in that time, but all that registered was another aneurysm. I was numb. *What just happened? How did this happen?* I now began to ask myself. I was not experiencing any headaches, no type of symptoms really. I tried to remember if I missed anything that could have signaled that something was wrong. I do remember that lately I had been forgetting more than usual. I knew this because when I asked my son to do something, his answer to me would be that already I asked many times and that he had already completed it a while ago.

"Boy I am getting old, leave me alone, it's age, these things happen when you are aging," I would say to him.

Then I began to dig further and with some recollection, one other occasion from several months prior had come to mind. I was at the gym doing front lunges with twelve pound weights in each hand, when suddenly I felt dizzy and lightheaded. I immediately stopped, went to the bathroom to wash my face, sat for a minute, then felt better and drove myself home, and that was that. Thinking then that I must have done too much in my workout, and my blood pressure or my blood sugar must have dropped too low. Here I was diagnosing myself as we nurses often do, instead of going to the doctor to check it out. I never imagined that it could be something worse developing. I teach my patients to report any and all symptoms experienced that are new to them to their doctors, and not to sit on it. Here I am not taking my own advice.

It was day two, and I was in the ICU. My son Kyle, my friend Robert, and Jennifer were in my room sitting. They were there when Dr. Lieu told me what they found and what they did. I looked up at their faces, and all I could see was three people who were close to me, in shock. I focused on my son's face. He looked so lost and confused. Just then, I realized I was not the only one hurting here. They were in as much pain and disbelief as I was. *What could I do to ease their pain?* I asked myself. I silently called upon God to give me the courage and strength to do what I was about to do. I wanted to show them that I was not in control, that God was, and wanted them to keep the faith. God saved me for his purpose and he would see me through this, but I had to do my part to help in the recovery. I then called out to Kyle.

"Kyle when you come to visit me tomorrow, please bring me some clothes, some of my dresses, my slacks, and my makeup bag, but make sure my lipstick is in it," I said. *This aneurysm does not have me, I have it, and I am going to fight it with every ounce of breath I have in my body,* I told myself.

"Robert and Jennifer, you guys need to go home and get some rest, you all have been here all night and day. I will be ok, I am in good hands. I am a former employee of this hospital and some of the staff knows me so they will take good care of me," I assured them.

They all left and I dozed off for a little bit after they left. When I awoke I saw my best friend, Candida, and her daughter Nicole standing at the side of the bed.

"Oh Roz, oh Roz! What happened Roz? You are the healthiest person I know," She said.

"How did you get here so quickly?" I asked. This had only happened yesterday.

"Kyle called and as soon as I saw it was Kyle's number and not yours I knew it had to be something wrong, because Kyle normally calls Nicole and not me. When he told me what happened and I heard the pain in his voice, I knew I had to be here right away, so we drove down," she said.

I lived in Maryland at this time and Candida lived in New York. We were neighbors when I lived in New York, and we became best friends. We have been best friends for over twenty years. She and Nicole spent some time with me in the hospital in D.C., then left and went to spend the night with Kyle at our home in Maryland. I am so blessed to have her in my life. *What a friend indeed*, I thought.

It was day three, and Kyle brought me my clothes and makeup bag. I was not so much of a makeup girl, however I did love to wear lip stick and eyeliner. When I received the bag I called my nurse Ramona, and asked her to get an order from the doctor for her to remove my foley catheter, a tube inserted in your bladder to drain urine, and to get me out of bed with bathroom privileges. *My patients are right,* I thought, *This foley was the most uncomfortable thing you could have inside you.* Now I was having a better perspective of a patient's life while in the hospital.

"You are on seizure precautions you know," Ramona said.

"Yes I know, but can I sit on the chair next to the bed and put pillows on both sides of the chair to protect my head in case of a seizure? I will be compliant. I will call for help, I promise not to get up by myself," I told her.

I just couldn't stay in that bed, my legs were getting weak and if I stayed in bed any longer I was afraid of becoming too stiff to move. My recovery would be faster if I could move.

"This body is made to move Ramona," I said. She smiled.

"Ok Rosalind, I will ask the doctor," She said. Not only did she ask him, she got him to come see me. Dr. Aulisi came, assessed me, and I asked him myself. He told me the foley could be removed, and I could now get out of bed with bathroom privileges.

This hospital is a teaching hospital. I worked there years ago as an RN in the cardiac intermediate care unit, or IMCU, so I was familiar with this hospital. My room was facing the nursing station, so I saw and heard most of what went on. I heard Ramona giving report one day to the oncoming nurse, telling her I was a nurse and had a lot of visitors, so they made some exceptions and allowed three people in my room at once instead of two. After Ramona got me up to the chair, I sat there for a while. While sitting, I glanced at the nursing station and saw a male resident who had also been doing rounds with the doctors earlier that day. I remember him telling me he was from Brazil. He waved at me and smiled, so I waved back. *Wow, what's going on here? I am sick, perhaps dying, and still there was some flirting going on. Boy I am very much alive, thank you Jesus!* I said to myself. The next day I got up early because I knew I was going to have a ton of visitors as news of me being hospitalized had spread, and I was blessed to have a lot of great friends.

I called my patient care technician and asked her to take me to the bathroom. I got myself cleaned, dressed in one of the dresses Kyle had brought for me, then put some face powder, lipstick, and eyeliner on. If you look good, you feel better, was my motto. I got back and sat on the chair next to the bed, and was ready for the day. Whatever the day would bring I would embrace it. My sister Agnes came, and I had her braid my hair so I could be fully groomed. My nurse Ramona walked in shortly after.

"Why are you dressed up and wearing makeup, where are you going?" Ramona said.

"Do you see that Brazilian doctor over there? I am checking him out," I said to her.

"You are so crazy," she said, and started laughing.

"I am alive honey and glad to be here, so I am going to live life like I had never live it before," I told her. I was so happy to be alive, knowing that a ruptured brain aneurysm was a killer and it did not kill me. It was a miracle and I was ready to get out and share this testimony with the world, and help others who may be going through similar or worse.

I have also been blessed with a sense of humor. My goal each day I am given breath of life is to make someone smile, so I do, and boy did I use it on the doctors and nurses during my hospitalization. I was told by several people everywhere I went that I looked like two famous people: Condoleezza Rice and Michelle Obama. It would depend on how I wore my hair that day. I got one or the other. I usually took it as a compliment and moved on. Day four in the Neuro ICU, and my nurse Ramona came into my room to do a neuro assessment on me and asked me to state my name.

"Today I am Michelle Obama, please tell the secret service I need my husband Barack now," I stated. The first time I said this to her she laughed so hard and loud that she must have forgotten she was in the ICU.

"You are too funny, you don't need to be in the ICU, you are doing too well. We have never had a patient like you here before. This is such a miracle and great to see," she said. That same day I had many of my former co-workers from Prince George's Hospital Center visit me.

"Never burn your bridges," my mother would say, so I did not.

I worked at PG Hospital Center in Maryland for ten years on a medical-surgical unit. On that unit we were a family, worked together, played together, so I became friends with most of my coworkers and treated all of them well and with respect. When I left, I left in good standing, and while some were not too pleased with my leaving, I had to move on. Even though we were like family and I made friends, I was not expecting to see or to be in touch with most of them after leaving. This is what amazed me that they even still thought of me and when they heard the news they showed up in groups, bearing gifts, offering prayers, and ready to lend a hand. When they saw me dressed in street clothes and makeup and sitting in the chair, they were confused, amazed, shocked, and happy all at the same time. They told me they definitely were not expecting to see me like this knowing the severity of the diagnosis.

"I was at St. Peter's door knocking, but he wouldn't let me in, and said I was too much for them to handle right now, so he sent me back to Earth to continue to give you guys hell. I was too greedy, I could not settle for just one, I had to go back for seconds. They found a second aneurysm, but this one is intact." They all laughed. Now I could joke about it somewhat, not only as I was feeling good, but because they were so serious and I had to let them know that it would be ok.

"Girl you have not changed, even in sickness you can make us laugh," They said.

As the days went by, I had so many visitors and so many prayers. Prayers were coming in from all parts of the world, Trinidad and Tobago, England, Canada, all of the U.S. and even as far as Japan. You would have thought I was famous. All the prayers and support from family and friends, the nurses, the hospital staff, and the doctors were all instrumental in my speedy recovery. I am a nurse, but now was on the other side of the fence as a patient. I was now in a unique position of having both perspectives, which gave me a better understanding of the nurse's job and how much we do on a daily basis, presenting me with a better appreciation of my career. It also allowed me to be more understanding and patient with my patients. The staff was all terrific. Teamwork is often emphasized in almost all healthcare institutions but is not always practiced. A lot of institutions are all talk and no action, but at this hospital, their spirit, communication, and work was exemplary. The right hand knows exactly what the left hand is doing, which makes so much of a difference for the patients. I was so impressed that I asked to speak to the director. When he came I told him he had an excellent team of workers in the neuro ICU.

"Treat them well, show your appreciation of them," I said.

"I will and I do, thank you for telling me this," He said.

Each day spent in the hospital I was improving, had no seizures, some tightness, aches and pain in my lower extremities and back, but no major complications. I was healing well. The doctors were testing me each day checking to see if the coiling was doing what it was meant to do. Less bleeding was noted each day as well as no swelling, which was good. Since I was now able to get out of bed, I was walking each day with either physical therapy or the nurses. I would ask my evening nurse, Tess, to take me for a walk in the evening if she was not too busy. She did, and looked forward to doing it with me each time she was at work. Sometimes I would ask them to dance with me, somehow I just wanted to get up and dance. Now it was the sixth day in the ICU, and the doctors had examined me. Their assessment was that I was good to be transferred out of the neuro ICU to the neuro IMCU and instead of the fourteen days he said I would be there, it was now looking like ten days total in the hospital. Having moved to the IMCU, I now shared a room with two other patients. Being with others in the IMCU, I sometimes forgot that I was there as a patient and not as a nurse, so I would go to the other two patients and help them. I became friends with one elderly lady who had a brain tumor removed and her entire head was bandaged. I would go over to her and help her with her meals, talk with her, and help with whatever I could until the nurses walked in and asked me to return to my side.

"Rosalind, you are here as a patient, not a nurse!" Ramona would say.

"I am bored and need to work, get me a uniform and put me to work please!" I would say. They all got to know me, so I got away with a little more than others.

While lying in the hospital for ten days, I did some serious thinking, reflection, and soul searching and came up with so many questions with very few answers. *Where do I go from here? What message is God sending me? Why was I saved? What's his purpose for me now? Was I truly taking good care of myself? Was I working too much? I recently got myself a second job only a month ago, did that contribute to this? What changes do I now have to make? Did I prepare my son enough so that he could function without me?* I knew he had been so dependent upon me lately. I did not have a will, nor did I have advance directives. Kyle would have been so lost if I had died. Oh boy, I had so much to do when I recovered. When I feel strong enough, I would have to sit with him, and go over so much stuff so that if this happened again we would both be better prepared.

It was now day ten, and I was up early as usual, dressed and waiting for my doctors. Here come the doctors.

"Ms. Noreiga, are you ready to go home? Everything looks good and we are discharging you home today with your son," They said.

Although I wanted to go home, somehow I was not celebrating when the time came. In the back of my head I knew that this bleeding around the brain was serious. And yes, the blood was reabsorbing after the coiling, but I knew that complication was still likely, and that I may not have been out of the woods quite yet. *Will the recovery be the same at home as it has been thus far?* I asked myself. Then I caught myself and told myself not to let the negative thoughts detour my progress. I was doing fine, and would continue to do fine as I kept the faith and continued to trust God. I got my discharge instructions, and Ramona informed the other staff of my discharge and many came by to say their goodbyes and wish me well. Even the director stopped by too. I ordered a large fruit basket from edible arrangements, and had it delivered to the staff on the unit, and we celebrated my speedy recovery.

Kyle drove me home and now he would be my caregiver for the next however many days until I was fully recovered. Could he do it, could he handled whatever came our way at home? It was so much for a young man his age to handled, he was not as strong as I am, I thought, but I taught him well and he has a good heart. He is a good kid and it will be ok I tried to tell myself. To my surprise when we got home, and Kyle pulled into the driveway, I got out of the car, and I saw my nurse friend Jackie waiting in her car in front of my home. Jackie and I were in nursing school together, and Jackie had a tendency to boss everyone around and sometimes acted like she was my mom, but she was a terrific friend.

"Rosie," She said, "let's go straight to your bed, and don't worry about anything. You have friends and we are here for you, we will help you."

She helped Kyle take me upstairs and into my bed. She also cooked and brought me food. What a blessing. I certainly was not alone in this as Jackie was not the only one who came by to help that day but many of my friends came by, and the day after, and the day after that until I was able to go back to work. They cooked, brought food did my shopping, cleaned my house, and some even helped with my mortgage, what a blessing.

"Give and it shall be returned to you
Good measure pressed down shaken together running over,
Will they pour into the fold of your garment
For the measure you measure with will be measured back to you."
Luke 6:28
This is how I live my life, giving and being a true friend to
others, I give and give unconditionally and it has returned
abundantly to me in a time when I needed it the most.

Friendship - A beautiful thing to have

A friend is
One who you can trust and depend on
The one that will ride the waves with you
One that when you are in need, is there, and always has your back
A friend will celebrate your success and encourage
you not to give up when you fail
A friend will be up front and straight forward
with you, will tell you the truth even at
times when you do not want to hear it.
A friend accepts and loves you for who you are
A friend can make you laugh even when
you don't feel like laughing
One that will pick you up when you are down
In the early hours of the morning when you
cannot sleep, when you are alone, afraid,
and have a lot on your mind, a friend is the one
who will not mind being woken up to
take your call, listen to you, tell you something
that will make you feel better, and
when you hang up, you can now fall asleep.
A friend is a gift and blessing, and everyone deserves one
Many people out there don't have any because
they simply don't know how to be one
It does not cost much to be a friend, but just a
little giving of yourself, however you
stand to gain so much when you become one.
A true friend is a lifeline that we all need,
everyone should have at least one to make
this journey of life a bit gentler, kinder, and happier, BE ONE.

Chapter 3

That Faithful Day part 3

My progress slowed somewhat once I got home. The first few days at home after being discharged from the hospital was difficult for me. I remember Dr. Armanda telling me to expect headaches, muscle spasms, and that seizures were highly likely, which is why he gave me seizure prescription meds for those. However, I had not experienced a headache or seizure up to this point. What I was experiencing was severe, excruciating pains from my lower back, mostly on the right side radiating to my right foot. Unable to get out of bed myself, it felt like sciatica nerve pain, which I had experienced many years ago. My legs and right side sometimes felt numb and paralyzed. I did not have any of these symptoms while in the hospital. I was determined to continue to fight this, so I tapped into my resources: my friends, some of whom were physical therapists and occupation therapists, and of course I used my dearest friend Robert, who was also a personal trainer. They all came at different times and worked with me. Here I was, learning proper balancing techniques, fine coarse motor coordination, and strength training. This was very helpful and within a few days I could feel and see the difference. I was making great progress.

I continued to welcome visitors on a daily basis at home. Friends prayed with me, laughed with me, fed me, and assisted with my household chores. I had so many visits, but unfortunately I could not remember all who visited me. My memory would come and then vanish. Nevertheless, I am very grateful and appreciate all who cared for me, supported me, prayed for me, and showed their love during this very trying time for me and my son. By the end of the first week at home, I was able to walk from my bedroom to downstairs on the first level. I was still unable to go in the room where this all happened. I still remembered the trauma of that day and had not yet found the courage to go into that room. My discharge instructions stated I had to meet with Dr. Armonda in two weeks.

It was now June 16th 2016, two weeks since being discharged from the hospital. My appointment with Dr. Armonda was scheduled for 2 pm at the Neurological Center at Washington Hospital Center in DC. My friend Jackie accompanied me to my appointment. Dr. Armonda thoroughly went over everything with me. He placed the CD of all my procedures into the computer, and explained in detail what I was looking at and what was done. He gave his prognosis and his recommendations for the second aneurysm. He informed me that in three months, he wants me to take another angiogram to check on the coiling of the first aneurysm and the size of the second aneurysm before planning for the craniotomy to clip the second aneurysm. Then we discussed how this might have happened. I informed him that all my life I lived a healthy lifestyle and only been sick with the flu yearly, which had been left untreated and that caused me to have viral cardiomyopathy, which has later been resolved by medications. I also informed him that I had been an athlete and a runner since I was twelve years old. From sprinting as a child, to long distance marathons as an adult, I had run several marathons until age fifty. I was neither a smoker nor a drinker, ate a healthy diet, mostly plant based foods, had never been hospitalized except for pregnancy and two emergency visits. The only doctor's office I visited maybe every two years was my gynecologist. Then why and how did this happen?

"What may have caused this?" I asked.

"The medical and neurological community does not know of a definite cause or findings. Some contributing factors we think are high blood pressure, congenital defects that may not have been detected as a child or in some cases genetic component. But they are not sure," He replied.

I informed him that I learned, only after this happened to me, of my first cousin having a brain aneurysm detected, after he complained of persistent severe headaches, and was treated for it with clipping. I also mentioned to him my concern for my son because he was scared and worried that he may experience the same. He informed me that it is difficult to say if my son would experience the same, and would advise him to seek urgent attention if he did experience headaches as well as to push for screening by CT scan or MRIs.

"Push hard because the insurance companies do not want to pay for routine MRI screening, that's why some doctors don't offer routine MRI screening based on family history," He stated.

"Well this is something we will have to fight the insurance companies for later on down the road, because this is a silent killer. If we can detect it early enough we can save lives," I said to him. He agreed. This is something I definitely intend to pursue. During our conversation, he then leaned forward, looked me directly in my eyes and said "Young lady if you were not physically fit and a healthy individual you would not have survived this rupture, and if I must say this myself, you are a walking living miracle. Not only did you survive it, you have no deficit or complications and your spirit is amazingly great, that is rare."

"Thank you Dr. Armonda. God has chosen one of the best neurological teams in the country to care for me. You had a hand in his miracle," I said. "Now when can I go back to work?" I asked.

"Everything looks good from my stand point, whenever you feel ready, you can," He said

"Ok. Can I have two more weeks at home, I don't feel quite ready," I said.

"Yes," he said, and signed my return to work form for me to return on June 28th, on light duty.

"Dr. Armonda you know there is no such thing as light duty in nursing when you are a staff nurse, especially on a very busy floor like oncology and orthopedics," I said

"You have to be careful, do what you can, do not push too fast; your body is still healing, sometimes the healing can take up to two years. Be careful," He said.

What Dr. Armonda did not know was that I had to put myself through my own test to determine my readiness for work, and that test was being able to dance. I love to dance and not just any dance, I must be able to do the wobble. In my head if I could do the wobble, I was ready to return to work. Every day I listen to the Tom Joyner Morning Show on the radio. Every Friday morning, from 8:00 am to 8:06 am, Tom will play V.I.C.'s "Wobble" song, sometimes mixed with the "Nay-Nay." I have been dancing to it every Friday that I am off from work, ever since he's been playing it.

It was now Friday, the end of the first week of my two weeks before returning to work. I got up early, got dressed, had my breakfast, and waited in my living room with the radio on the Tom Joyner Show, waiting for the wobble. 8:00 am came and I turned up the volume. I stood up, and began to dance the wobble, but being very careful. I quickly realized that my soul and spirit was willing, but my body was not ready, and I still felt a little weak. I could tell I was not doing it the way I normally danced the wobble. Instead I was doing it the way a hundred year old body would do it. But I was happy I attempted and did something. Did that stop me from trying again? No, it did not. The next week I continued to work on some of the exercises given to me by my personal trainer friends and Robert, and was beginning to feel stronger. My balance and coordination was improving, still no seizure activity, the muscle was more relaxed and the pain had subsided.

It was now Friday of the second week, and I had to return to work on Monday. It was time for me to again attempt to wobble. It was 8:00 am, the wobble was blasting on the Tom Joyner Morning show, and I was dancing, and this time, I was doing it. I was doing the wobble. All the way down to the floor, and back up I was succeeding, I was into it, pumped, feeling good, and enjoying it. My son was sitting on the stairs looking at me like I was crazy.

"Mom are you ok, I can't believe you are doing this," He said.

"This is it baby, I am doing it, I can do it, yes I can, I am back, and I am ready to return to work," I said. He then walked away laughing and shaking his head. After dancing the wobble like I normally do, I felt so good, so energized, and so positive of my outcome going forward. *It's amazing how far you can go when you put your mind into something and put faith in God, you can truly move mountains,* I thought. After this experience, I now view life in a new perspective, and I am going to live it to the fullest. I came too close to losing it, not to enjoy it.

It was Monday, June 28th, 2016, thirty five days after suffering a ruptured brain aneurysm, and I was returning to work on a hectic floor: the oncology and orthopedic unit. If that's not a miracle, then I don't know what is. I drove myself on the twenty minute drive to work. I got to the floor, and received the warmest welcome back, lots of hugs and smiles from my coworkers and colleagues, my family away from home.

We huddled and prayed, giving God thanks. Michelle was one of the Patient Care Technicians, (PCT), on my floor and a very good worker. We worked well together.

"Rosalind welcome back, and by the way my boyfriend says hello," She said.

"Your boyfriend, do I know your boyfriend, and how does he know I was sick?" I asked.

"When he came home from work that night that you had the emergency, he told me he just transported a nurse that works at my hospital to Washington Hospital Center, and since we were informed about it on the job, I told him that's Rosalind, and she works on my floor. He was your flight nurse who took care of you in the helicopter," She said.

"The guy with the great biceps, triceps, and great upper body? That very fit looking guy is your boyfriend?" I repeated.

"Yes," she said.

"Michelle, I hardly remember much during this entire ordeal, but I specifically remember him. Michelle, girl, I perhaps was dying, but I was checking him out," I said. Michelle laughed out loud. "Please tell him thanks for taking such good care of me and for his part in the rapid response when I was down," I said to her.

"I will tell him," She said. *Wow! This is such a small world,* I thought. I was so astonished when Michelle told me this.

"You lived a healthy lifestyle, you exercise so much, you eat healthy, and you still have gotten sick. I will continue to sit my fat ass down and eat what I want, no exercise for me, what's the point?" Another nurse said to me. We all laughed.

"No one is immune from illness or death. Exercise and eating a healthy balanced meal, abstaining from too much alcohol, smoking and drugs, is what saved my life. If I had poisoned my body with those things, and did not exercise as I did, my outcome might have been quite different. God gives us life and an incredible anatomy that we should treat as our temple. We have got to take care of it and remember God helps those who help themselves. We've got to meet God halfway. I did, and the rest is history," I said.

At Washington Adventist Hospital I worked the twelve hour day shift, three days per week. They allowed self scheduling at the hospital, however it was not guaranteed that you would get the days you selected. Before returning to work, I spoke to the unit manager/assistant director Sonia, informing her that I would not be able to work consecutive days and asked to be scheduled to work every other day, giving myself a day between those long twelve hour shifts to rest as my body was still healing. Although highly functional at this point, I knew those long days could be very tedious on the body, and knowing that I just had a major medical event, I wanted to be careful not to push my body over the limit. Sonia thankfully was very understanding and empathetic to my needs, therefore she scheduled me to work every other day, and that was very helpful.

"I got your back Rosalind, don't worry, we will take care of you," She said.

I was functioning on the job without problems, and no complications. I was functioning so well no one could tell from just looking at me that I recently was so close to death by suffering and recovering from a ruptured brain aneurysm.

After having experience being a patient in the hospital for a period of time, I now had a new perspective. I began to notice the difference in my care for my patients. I found that I had become more patient, a better listener than I had been before, especially with the patients that provided a greater challenge. I now had a better understanding of their needs, and was able to identify with them. After having gone through the first round of this two part aneurysm and survived, I was now able to use this platform to share my testimony with others to help them get through their ordeal, especially those who were having a difficult time coping with their diagnosis and treatment plan. I now find myself spending more time teaching my patients, educating them of preventive measures in taking better care of their health. Those who have not reached the acceptance stage in their grief, and are still angry have a tendency to take it out on the staff. I took the extra time to sit with them, hold their hands, and share my story with them, encouraging them not to give up, keep the faith, to trust that God will see them through as he has me, according to his will for them. What I have noticed when I share my story with them, is that I get the most astonishing looks.

"You recently had what? And you are alive? And you are back at work so soon and with a smile, and caring for me?" They would say. After sharing my story, and encouraging them to keep the faith, I saw more positive attitudes in their behavior and more willingness not to give up, but to continue the fight. I remember one patient on the verge of giving up that I shared my story with who, after hearing my story, was inspired to fight, instead of staying in bed and feeling sorry for herself. She decided to get up, be compliant with her care plan, and worked harder to get out of the hospital. And within a couple of days she did. Two days after she was discharged from my unit, she wrote an email to the director of the unit, thanking the staff for the great care she received.

"I want to especially thank the nurse who had the ruptured aneurysm for my speedy recovery. I do not remember her name, but I remember her story, because her story inspired me," She mentioned in the email.

When the director called me into her office, I first thought I might be in trouble, then she showed me the email and I smiled. It felt so good that I made a difference in this patient's life. If I can use my story to help others, this is all worth it I thought to myself.

Chapter 4

That Faithful Day part 4

I continued to work every other day as scheduled, functioning well, now incorporating time to relax. I was discharged from the hospital on the second day of June, 2016, after spending ten days there. It was the first week in July, and I now received a billing statement from the hospital. It stated the cost for my stay at the hospital, excluding the physician's bill, was one hundred and eighty thousand dollars. I looked at it and laughed so hard I almost wet myself. I laughed because I was saying to myself, *I just suffered a ruptured brain aneurysm, and it did not kill me, I will be damned if I let this bill give me a heart attack and kill me.* I gently put it down. I worked as a staff bedside nurse and did not have any dealings with the financial aspect of the hospital, and had no experience with billing; therefore I did not know the cost of a hospital stay like mines.

My first thought was this is a mortgage. Then I took a closer look at the bill and noticed that some of the services they charged me for I did not receive. I will admit that I was very happy and appreciated the excellent care I received at the hospital, but the billing was off. *I would not stress over this,* I told myself. I would let the insurance company deal with this. Two weeks after receiving the billing statement, I received a statement from my health insurance informing me that they declined the payment to the hospital due to lack of documents needed that was omitted by the hospital. Bottom line, the hospital did not fulfill the necessary requirements in order for the bill to be properly processed. Now where did that leave me? It left me in a fight between the hospital and the insurance company. Here I was trying to recover, having to work to pay my house mortgage and bills, and I was stuck with another bill. Here I was not able to pay this bill and did not want it messing up my credit. I got on my knees and prayed for help. Then, one day out of the blue, I received a call from a nurse Millie, saying she was the nurse coordinator, an RN from Conifer Solutions: my health insurance. She was assigned to my case, and was here to help me with post-up care as well as act as a liaison between the hospital and the insurance company to resolve the issue with my bill. She informed me that the health cnsurance Companies are now using RN's to help resolve billing issues and post hospitalization issues that patients experience after discharge. After hearing this, I looked up above me and said in silence to my God, *You did it again, this time you did not come yourself, but you send me an Angel (Millie). Thank you God!* I said.

Millie began to work immediately on getting this issue resolved. She was communicating back and forth between the hospital billing department, the insurance company, and me.

"Rosalind," She said, "I am going to do my part, but I need you to call the hospital appeals department as well and ask them to appeal this decision by the insurance company, because if they don't appeal, you will end up having to pay all of it yourself." I did as Millie asked me to. I called the billing department, and asked them for appeals. They reviewed my chart and informed me that there was nothing to appeal because my account showed a zero balance.

"That could not be true," I said, "are you sure." It was a man that I was speaking to from the hospital billings department.

"Yes you have a zero balance," He said. I asked him to please send me a copy of that statement that was showing a zero balance. He said he would. I continued to receive bills from the physicians billing department and what I could pay, I paid. Millie checked in with me two times a week to see how I was progressing. When she next called I informed her that I called the hospital's billing department and they informed me that I now had a zero balance. I also informed her of some of the physician's bills that I paid. Millie did not buy that, she was skeptical.

"Are you sure? This must be a mistake," She kept saying. "I will try appeals again. Do not pay any bill until this is settled, because you might be paying more than you should. If the insurance rejects the hospital bill they will not pay for the physicians as well," She told me.

This whole billing thing was such a mess and I was caught in the middle of it while trying to recover. I was paying around four hundred and fifty dollar per month for insurance. I had been paying health insurance for such a long time, living a healthy lifestyle as a preventive measure to keep me from having to need to use the insurance. I had not had a health claim for the past ten years, and now that I needed it, they were giving me a hard time. But I was determined not to let them deter my progress in healing. Millie kept telling me to call the hospital appeals department one more time to verify the zero balance. I called again, this time I got a female attendant.

"I don't believe this, I don't believe this!" I could hear her saying to herself.

"What don't you believe?" I asked.

"We did not do what we were supposed to do and as a result we have to eat the cost of your stay with us. So yes, you do have a zero balance on your statement," She said. Now that two staff members of the hospital billing department confirmed a zero balance, I could breathe easy. I asked her to send me a copy of the statement with a zero balance as well and she informed me that the computer was showing that a copy was sent to my home address.

"Thank you!" I said to her then I shouted "Thank you Jesus!" I called Millie and informed her. She was still confused and remained skeptical. I told her for now I will go along with it. "We will see when I returned to the hospital for my second surgery in December 2016," I said to Millie.

Chapter 5

That Faithful Day part 5

One day, in February, 2016, it was my off day from work. This day I chose to do absolutely nothing but just eat and lay in bed. My lazy day, I called it. I was in bed relaxing when a thought came to mind. *Why don't you take a vacation this summer?* Now I did not feel stressed, or tired, or as though I needed a vacation, but this thought existed and I acted upon it. I immediately phoned my niece Cathy Ann who lived in Trinidad and Tobago, and had a managerial position in one of the oil companies there. She travels all over the world on business, plus she is one that does not hesitate to take vacation.

"Cathy, where are you vacationing this year?" I asked. She told me that she and her family would be vacationing in West Palm Beach Florida, and would be staying at her husband Nigel's uncle's place. They would be there from July 22nd through July 30th. "Could I vacation with you guys?" I continued.

"Sure, it will be good to see you." She said. Ok, then it was West Palm Beach Florida for me. After hanging up from her I went to my computer, got on my job's website, and applied for one week vacation from July 22nd through July 28th, 2016. Now all this was taking place in

February. I did not foresee, nor imagine that I would have a ruptured brain aneurysm on May twenty third and that this vacation would be needed in July as part of my therapy and healing. As I tried to put the pieces together, my only conclusion to all this was that it must be God telling me that he had a different plan for me. He knew this aneurysm was coming. It was the Holy Spirit talking to me this entire time and I was so unaware, until after that faithful day when everything began to unfold. Now I was born and raised in the Catholic faith. I always believed in God, and tried to live a good life being considerate to others and in accordance with His teaching and in obedience to the Ten Commandments, as I was taught. I will not say I am a born again or devoted Christian, nor do I have a strong knowledge of the scriptures in the Bible. But this whole thing was mind boggling and scary to me. So many questions arose. As I continued to gather the pieces, I kept thinking that this might be God's way of showing me that he wanted me closer to him. I must say this was quite an awakening for me, that I truly welcomed.

Surprisingly within two days I received an email from my director at work informing me that my vacation request had been approved. Without delay I booked a flight in February to West Palm Beach. Now I was set for a vacation that I had no idea would be so needed and welcomed. After being in work for three weeks after hospitalization of the first aneurysm, it was time to take a now deserving therapeutic vacation.

It was July 22nd, 2016. I was flying from Maryland to West Palm Beach. It was time to board my flight, but I waited a minute because I had titanium in my head, the material used to coil the aneurysm. *Would the alarm go off at the security check point?* I asked myself. I did ask my neurosurgeon if I was clear to travel by air, and he assured me it was ok. Here I was hoping I did not cause a scene at check point, and I did not.

The alarm did not go off and I had an uneventful flight. *Amen,* I kept saying to myself. I got to the hotel, got into the room, only to discover that it was a luxury suite, with a huge bedroom, a walk in bathroom, a hot tub, a kitchen, and huge living room space. *It's a complete one bedroom apartment,* I thought. It was overlooking the outdoor pool and water park. What a nice room. The hotel had great restaurants, indoor and outdoor pools, gym, spa, shops, and its own private beach. There were restaurants and bars on the beach. It was so beautiful, I felt as though I was on my honeymoon, except without the man. Each day I awoke and after having breakfast, and before going to bed at night, I would take long walks on the beach. Listening to the sound of the ocean and watching the waves relaxed me. You know that voice that I have been talking about, it returned. *This is your next destination,* I kept hearing it echo, over and over again. I had not entertained a thought of Florida being my next home or my retirement destination, but this voice was telling me it is. Needless to say, I enjoyed the vacation in West Palm Beach.

One day during this vacation, while sitting in the cabana on the beach sipping my virgin pina colada, I was talking on the phone with my cousin Sheila, who lived in Boston. While talking, I could hear the music that was playing in the bar on the beach. On the speakers I could hear a Calypso by the Lord Kitchener, a famous Calypsonian, from Trinidad and Tobago. I am from Trinidad and Tobago, the land of steel pan and calypso, the land with the greatest carnival on earth, and here I was hearing an old calypso called "Sugar Bum Bum." In the song he is speaking of a woman's big butt and how it looks when she is walking, admiring it. But the song has such a great rhythm. It's so rhythmic; you just can't sit still when it is playing. It just makes you want to get up and shake your butt. So I did.

"They are playing Kitchener's Sugar Bum Bum, and I am shaking mines on the beach while everyone around is looking at me and smiling," I said to Sheila. It had been such a long time since I had heard that calypso, so I went to the bar attendant and asked him to replay it, and he did, and this time other people who were on the beach joined me in dancing to the beat. It was so much fun. I felt like I was in Trinidad.

"I am from the land of steel band and calypso, so it was only fitting that I represented my country," I said to Sheila, she laughed.

Cathy, Nigel, and their daughter Jade visited me at the hotel. We spent some time together on the beach and the pool, and we all had so much fun. My stress levels, which my neurosurgeon told me to keep at minimal, was at zero. *This was exactly what the doctor ordered*, I thought. This at times felt so surreal. One minute I was at my darkest hour and the next minute I was dancing on the beach under the beautiful skies and calming seas. How beautiful life was that I had taken all this for granted. *Now that I am still in this world I am going to cherish and appreciate all the beauty that surrounds me*, I said to myself.

After returning to my home in Maryland from a very well deserved and fabulous vacation, I began to give serious thought to what that voice was saying to me while on the beach in West Palm. I now seriously began to believe that this was God's direction for me. This might be the perfect time to cut the umbilical cord from Kyle. Leaving him on his own will give him an opportunity to stand on his own two feet and to grow. I went on the internet and began to search for condos for sale in West Palm Beach Florida, those closest to the water since the water had been so calming for me. I guess my ultimate goal was to reduce my stress levels and this would be the perfect way to do so. This meant I had to sell my home in Maryland, and move once again. But it would have to be done after my second surgery and would depend on how well I progressed after the surgery. I would have to discuss this with Kyle and my friend Robert. I thought to myself.

I continued to work while healing and at the same time preparing for aneurysm round two, (craniotomy), before year's end. But before doing so I had to take another cerebral angiogram to check on the coiling of the ruptured aneurysm and the size of the second one. My angiogram with Dr. Lieu was scheduled for mid September. An angiogram is a minimally invasive test that uses X-rays and an iodine-containing contrast material to produce images of blood vessels in the brain. In cerebral angiography, a thin plastic tube, also known as a catheter, is inserted into an artery in the leg or arm through a small incision in the skin. It was September 16th, and I was in the hospital again for an angiogram. My son took me and stayed with me. He was with me all the way; he is going through this as much as I was. Needless to say I was thankful and grateful that he was with me. The angiogram was performed by Dr. Lieu, my favorite neuroradiologist, and it went well. He later informed me that the coiling was intact and doing what it was meant to do, and the second aneurysm was also intact and had not changed in size. I was hoping to hear that it was no longer there, but Dr. Lieu must have read my mind.

"It is still there, it does not just disappear you know," He said to me.

"What do you recommend I do now?" I asked. He informed me that I had to discuss treatment with Dr. Armonda, but also stated he will clip it to prevent the chances of rupturing in the future. Two weeks later I met with Dr. Armonda the neurosurgeon. We discussed treatment and he also recommended that I get it clipped based on the fact that I now have a history of one rupturing, and being an active, still fairly young individual, it was the best option in his opinion. My birthday was approaching and I did not want to be in the hospital nor in bed around my birthday simply because I treat my birthday as a national holiday. It's all about me celebrating myself. I decided that I would do the surgery, however, it must be done after my birthday I informed him. He then advised me to have it done before year's end. I celebrated my birthday with my friend Carlene whose birthday is the day after mines. We went to a club near my home and danced the night away. While on the dance floor a guy asked me to dance. I danced with him not holding on each other, just in front of each other. The song that we were dancing to says "Drop it low," so I was dancing all the way to the floor which I love to do.

"Do not hesitate to call 911 if I'm unable to get back up," I said to him. He looked at me confused, so I just laughed and continued dancing.

It's time to have a talk with Kyle. After meeting with the surgeon and deciding on the surgery I sat my son down to discuss our situation and where do we go from here. We went over where all my personal and financial belongings and assets are located. We discussed advance directives, a will that I still had to make, what I wanted done if and when I could not speak for myself, and we even discussed what to do in case I die. Kyle was very uncomfortable with this. I could tell by his uneasiness.

"Mom are we seriously doing this, do we have to do this now," He said. I informed him that this is our new reality that we have to face together and that it's time he moved from the denial stage to the acceptance stage because it was already here. And yes, we were doing this. It had been my son and I in the absence of his father for over nineteen years of his life and he had become so dependent upon me for almost everything. He was an only child. My sister, his aunt, lived in Maryland too, but he was not close with her so it is mainly just him and I. I was thankful that God had blessed him with some great friends as well. I had not prepared him before this and believed now was the time to do so because if I didn't, I knew he would be quite lost if I died during surgery.

I had mentioned that God had placed resources in each of our lives for a purpose. Sometime we are too proud to call upon these resources when in need. As stubbornly independent as I am, I try not to be too proud. Therefore I have a list of my closest friends, the people I know I can rely upon through thick or thin. This list is placed on every refrigerator wherever my place of residence may be for Kyle to see and use in case of emergency. I must say when this happened, that faithful day, he did use this list, and called everyone on this list to inform them of what happened to me. In doing so, he received so much help he never imagined he would receive. All the people on this list that he called all came through for us both. I was reminded that when we live an unselfish and giving life it will be returned abundantly, and it had for me. Kyle, if he did not learn that before, this experience must have taught him a very valuable lesson that I am sure he will not forget for it has changed him as well. I began to see a more mature child. He now shows concern, he was involved in my care, for the first time I saw an unselfish, compassionate, and empathetic child. He gave up time with his friends to care for me. He would now come home directly from work, to check on me. Each time he passed by my bedroom door he would ask if I was ok, and what he could do for me. God has a way of turning things around, and he sure has in my case, and I am so grateful for it all.

Chapter 6

Aneurysm #2

Before scheduling the surgery, I had to make sure that the hospital and the neurosurgical department informed the insurance company and sought approval for the surgery as well as supplied all the appropriate documents needed so that they can be paid. I did not want to have to go through the stress of billing like the first time around. They assured me they did. The craniotomy to clip the second aneurysm was scheduled for November 30th, 2016 at seven in the morning. The hospital instructed me to report to admitting at 5:00 am. What is aneurysm clipping? "The goal of surgical clipping is to isolate an aneurysm from the normal circulation without blocking off any small perforating arteries nearby. Under general anesthesia, an opening is made in the skull, called a craniotomy. The brain is gently retracted to locate the aneurysm. A small clip is placed across the base, or neck, of the aneurysm to block the normal blood flow from entering. The clip works like a tiny coil-spring clothespin, in which the blades of the clip remain tightly closed until pressure is applied to open the blades. Clips are made of titanium and remain on the artery permanently," According to http://www.mayfield clinic. com/PE-Clipping.htm . This surgery can take from three to six hours.

Now that I had a date for the surgery, I had to apply for the Family and Medical Leave Act (FMLA) at my job. I was fairly new at this hospital. After the first aneurysm, which was an emergency, I had to go on leave of absence, and was not qualified for FMLA since I was there less than a year. I was placed on short term disability which only paid me fifty percent of my salary while I was on leave. Financially, it was a bit of a struggle with all the bills due, but I did not worry about it. Thankfully I received helped from family and friends. I applied and was approved for FMLA for two months leave after my surgery. Having discovered the problem and knew its treatment, it was approached differently by me and my son. We were now better prepared emotionally, physically, and spiritually for the surgery and whatever came after. All my friends and family were on board with prayers and whatever I needed. *I am truly blessed,* I thought. The last day of work before beginning my FMLA, I informed my co-workers of my pending surgery and my only concern was that my hair would have to be shaved. I was terrified that I would have to wear a wig. I have beautiful hair and did not want to lose it. Terry, the charge nurse, heard my conversation about the hair.

"I could smack you. You are going for major surgery that may have major complications, one that is very risky, you can lose your life and your only concern is your hair?" She said.

"Yes that's my only concern," I said. I had already made my peace with God and trust in his will for me.

On November 29th, at 6:00 pm, less than twelve hours before my scheduled surgery, I received a phone call from someone from the hospital's billing department, a female attendant, informing me that I would need to bring five thousand dollars when I come to the hospital the next day before the surgery could be performed.

"What?" I asked, "Is this your policy? I have not heard of this before,

and besides my surgery is less than twelve hours away, where I am going to get five thousand dollars at this time?" I continued.

"Then you will have to reschedule," She said.

"Oh hell to the no. The surgeon and his team are already prepared,
everything is in place for this surgery, I am not re-scheduling, I will
be there at five in the morning tomorrow and something will have to
be worked out," I said to her and hung up. *If this is God's will for me it
will happen and the devil is not going to stop it,* I thought. It is the most
disgusting thing in my opinion when money becomes priority over
a person's life. Here I am trying to save my life and her only concern
was about money. *How did we as a people get to this point, lost compassion,
become so cold?* I continued to ask myself. I understand that I have to
pay for my care and have in the past, but informing me on such short
notice before my surgery is inappropriate and insensitive. I did not inform Dr. Armonda of this, knowing that if I did he would be furious,
and I certainly did not want to cause any problems. I got there the next
morning, November 30th, 2016 at 5:00 am and had the most friendly,
understanding, and helpful admitting clerk. He offered several options
and came up with a payment plan that I could afford and the surgery
was on as schedule.

It was 6:00 am, and I was in the pre-operative area of the hospital
going through my instructions with the nurses, the anesthesiologist,
the surgeons, and his assistants. Before reaching this point I had already
done some research on this type of surgery and was equipped with
some knowledge of what it entailed. However I was surprised and a
bit shocked to learn from Dr. Armonda that at times it is difficult to
replace the bone that they will be removing to get to the aneurysm and
if that happens, he will have to store it into my stomach and reattempt
to replace it at a later date. I was ok with everything else until I learned
of this, and for a minute, negative energy began to float around me. I

soon learned that the Holy Spirit, who was with me, was stronger than the devil that was putting this negative thought in my mind, so I silently began to pray and continued to put my faith and trust that God would bring me through it all.

Kyle was with me in the pre-op area and heard everything the surgical team told me. As a child he was raised in a Catholic church, and we often prayed together while he was growing up. However, as an adult he moved away from that, and I was not sure if he still prayed or believe in God anymore, but I asked him to pray with me, and he did. I also knew at this very time all my friends and family who had knowledge of the time of surgery were also praying for me. I knew I was pretty much prayed up at this point and good to go.

It was 7:00 am now, and they were wheeling me into the operating room. Kyle had to say his goodbye at this point, so he let go of my hands, and gave me a kiss.

"Whatever happens in there, you will be ok. I gave you the tools for life, use it, you are stronger than you think," I told him.

Now I was in the operating room, placed on the operating table. As I looked around the room, all I could see was a sea of blue. The operating room staff was dressed in their blue caps, gowns, footies, and gloves. There were so many of them in the room, I am not sure of the exact number, but I remember I counted twelve. *These are my twelve Angels, I am in good hands, I can close my eyes now, I will be ok,* I said to myself. And I did, and the next time I opened them roughly twelve hours later, I was again happy to be in this world.

The first thing I did after opening my eyes was lift my gown to check my stomach, to see if he opened it to place the bone. I guess that was still heavy on my mind. They did not.

"Thank you God," I shouted. When Dr. Armonda next came to see me, he explained to me how the surgery went, and the success in replacing the bone. The surgery itself took six hours. Once again I was blessed to be alive. Two major neurological events within six months, and I was still here in this world without any deficits to tell about it, what a miracle. I was so proud to be one of God's miracles.

After this surgery, I stayed one day in the Intensive Care Unit and three days in IMCU, and then I was discharged to home. I had a drain placed in my head to remove the fluid, which was removed twenty four hours after the surgery. He did a very nice cut at the side of my head and did not remove much hair. The incision was about eight inches in length, and staples were placed to close the area. I was so thankful for that cut. I did not have to wear a wig after all. My hair on the left side was long enough to brush over to the right side to cover the incision. I was pretty much on bed rest for twenty four hours. This surgery was easier for me to deal with mostly because it was planned and we were better prepared. Although it came with higher risk of infection, and seizure activities were highly likely, I was doing better than expected. I was up and walking the next day, in good spirits. I continued to use my sense of humor on the nurses and doctors. As a nurse, I try to develop a relationship with my patients. This builds trust and also promotes healing, and as a patient I try to do the same, making it easier for all. I had a male nurse at night and did not remember his name, but I remember how good he was to me and how great of a nurse he was. One night he came in and found me out of bed walking in my room.

"Why aren't you in bed?" He said.

"Because I want to dance, dance with me," I said. I was teasing him.

"Rosalind, I can't dance. Don't you see I am white, white people do not have rhythm," He said to me.

"We all can dance, dancing is about feeling the music, both the mind and body feeling the music, however and whatever part of your body feels the music you move that part, there is no wrong or right way, it is individualized. It's simple, let me show you," I said.

"My partner will love you for saying that, because he loves to dance and always wants me to dance with him," he said.

Life is so short. No one knows that better than I do at this point, therefore it is so important to enjoy it. I was so happy to be alive, and just wanted to show and share that happiness by making everyone around me feel happy as well. The nurse must have mentioned the dancing to Dr. Armonda because when Dr. Armonda came to discharge me the next day, he came with some residents and interns, as this was a teaching hospital.

"Rosalind I am discharging you home today with your son and no dancing for at least two weeks," He said. I looked at him, trying for a second to figure out how best to address this with him with a sense of humor.

"Dr. Armonda, please have someone shine your best shoes, because I am taking you dancing tonight!" I said to him. The residents and interns with him began to laugh. Dr. Armonda, who also had a sense of humor, smiled and his face turned slightly red.

"You are doing exceptionally, and amazingly great, take care of yourself, and keep up that spirit, I will see you in two weeks to remove the staples," He said to me.

The healing continues at home taking one day at a time. This time around I am feeling and doing much better than after the first surgery. Within a day after being home, I was able to take walks in my neighborhood by myself without any distress. I am a very independent, and a hardworking person who is constantly active. As I was restricted, given limitations for a couple weeks, it was so difficult for me to be compliant. It was hard for me to feel good, and not be able to do anything. If I did not want complications or setbacks, I needed to obey. So

I did, to a point. It was the month of December and the holidays were approaching. I was not big on Christmas celebrations anymore because it has become too commercialized, and the Christ in Christmas has been removed. But I tried to do what I could to help others by giving to charitable organizations. My credit union has a coat drive for disabled children, and the date was fast approaching. Only two days away, but the doctor said I was not able to drive for two weeks. My friends were very busy, and I truly did not want to have them go out of their way to accommodate my needs, and my son had to work. I was truly blessed and wanted so much to share that blessing. I had to make it to this coat drive myself on December 9th, 2016. I felt good. The weather was beautiful. By mid-day, I decided to go to Burlington Coat Factory, two miles from my home, and purchased two beautiful coats for two teenagers, one boy, and one girl. Then I drove myself to the credit union to deliver them. I drove slowly, being mindful that if I should have even one symptom that was out of the normal, I would immediately pull over and call for help. Thank God that did not happen and I got there safely. Santa Claus was at the credit union taking pictures with the kids for the coat drive. After I put my coats in the collection box, I was asked by one of the bank employees if I wanted a picture with Santa. Of course I said yes. I sat on Santa's lap and two pictures were taken. While sitting on his lap he asked if I was a good girl this year.

"No, I am being naughty right now because I am disobeying the doctor's orders. I just had surgery and should not be driving but I did it anyway just to come here. Please do not tell my doctor," I said to Santa. He looked at me like I was a crazy person that had just escaped from a mental institution.

"Your secret is safe with me," He smiled and said. After leaving the coat drive, I went to Costco, about a two minute drive away, to get a few things. Then I drove myself home. I got home safely. After settling in, I went to bed to relax. To my surprise the phone was ringing and it was my neighbor across the street Ms. Lisa. She and I had become friends.

"I know you know that you shouldn't be driving, why are you so hard headed, and you were gone for three hours," She said to me. I laughed.

"Besides spying on me, you are timing me too?" I said.

"You need to rest," She continued. She was not the only one who showed concern and voiced their dissatisfaction with my behavior. Another friend scolded me via text. I have never been scolded via text before. I text her, asking her jokingly to take me dancing.

"You are not a robot, you need to give your body a chance to heal. Sit your little butt down and read a book or research something on the internet," She replied back. I thought this was amusing because I was doing fine.

"I am not a robot, all this time I thought I was. Ok mommy, I'll sit my tiny butt down," I texted her back. It was not that I was trying to be defiant, I was truly feeling great. It was amazing and a miracle I was enjoying, but my friends and family were confused and probably did not understand it. This was such a great time for me. Each morning that I awoke, and my feet touch the floor, I became ecstatic, so happy to be in this world, and physically I was feeling strong. I did not have any deficits, and what a blessing.

It was now the middle of December, two weeks after my craniotomy, and the staples that closed my incision had to be removed. I had to visit Dr. Armonda. Before going to his office, I decided to get some goodies for him and his staff as it was the holidays, and Christmas was fast approaching. I picked up some food and drinks for his office staff, and some bottles of wines as a thank you and a holiday gift for Dr. Armonda and Dr. Lieu, the two fabulous doctors that God had appointed to perform this miracle that just gave me a new life. My son drove me to his office, which was also at the hospital. After greeting the staff and thanking them for all the hard work they did, I gave them the food. Dr. Armonda met me and took me to his exam room.

"Whatever it is that you are doing, keep doing it, because you are looking great," He said to me. He then removed the staples from my head and said it is healing nicely. He asked me if I drove myself here, and I informed him that my son drove me but stepped outside for a minute. He went on to ask if I drove anytime within this two week period.

"Dr. Armonda I will not lie to you, I did drive myself to a charity event," I said to him. He asked what distance and I told him it was a ten mile roundtrip. He said that it was ok and asked how it I felt while driving. I told him I was fine. I then showed him my picture with Santa.

"I brought this gift for you and Dr Lieu. I do not know how to get it to Dr. Lieu, can you give it to him for me?" I said.

"Why don't I call him over, he will be so happy and surprised to see how well you are doing," Dr. Armonda said. He called him over and within a few minutes Dr. Lieu arrived. He was beaming with smiles.

"Look at you, look at you. You had two neurosurgical procedures within six months and you look so good, what have you been doing?" He said.

"Dancing!" I teased. Dr. Armonda then handed him the gift which was two bottles of wine.

"What's this? It's party time," He said.

"Dr. Armonda prohibited me from dancing, so I figured I would use reverse psychology on him. If I can get him drunk after drinking the wine, then he might be impaired enough to join me in salsa dancing. Dr. Lieu, come dance salsa with me," I said. To my surprise he started dancing with me in the office. The office was closed to patients at this time and I was his last patient.

"Dr. Lieu I think we will have to take dancing lessons so we can go dancing with Rosalind," Dr. Armonda said. After Dr. Lieu left, Dr. Armonda asked me if I was on Facebook, but my reply was no. I asked why, and he said he would like to do a documentary on my story. I did not feel quite up to the task at the time so I regretfully declined. He then then informed me that together with Dr. Lieu and his patient care coordinator Lisa, they ran an aneurysm support group every third Wednesday of each month, and he wanted me to come to the group and tell my story. I promised him I would do that.

Dr. Armonda, Dr. Lieu, and I developed a good doctor/client relationship that is unique, respectable, and special. I trusted them with my life. I would trust them with my son's life without a doubt. This is the rewarding path of being in the medical/nursing field, when you get to see the progress the patient has made, and the joy on their faces when they make it out alive, or can leave the hospital independently like in my case. I came in unconscious with a diagnosis that has a high probability of death, and death did not occur. And they were instrumental in me walking out of the hospital alive, without any issues, and in great spirit. To me, there is nothing more rewarding than that. I experienced this a few times in my nursing career.

Chapter 7

Healing Continues

After the craniotomy and getting discharged from the hospital, I was off work for two months. I had to return to Dr. Armonda in one year for another angiogram, to check on the aneurysm clipping and coiling. This time around I planned not only to rest more, but to take more walks and do more physical exercises to regain my strength. It was winter and I would have to return to work soon. My biggest concern was driving thirty minutes to work, especially when it snows. Doctor's Community, the hospital the paramedics took me to when this first happened, was five minutes from my home. I had been trying to get a position there for quite some time now, but had been unsuccessful. I decided to try one more time, as it would have been so helpful to me. I went on their website to search for vacant positions and to my surprise there were a few. I applied for a position in their observation unit and would wait and see what happened. Christmas was fast approaching. I was going to spend Christmas with my best friend Candida and her family, my second family, in New York this year. Dr. Armonda advised me not to drive, but agreed that the train was a better alternative.

On December 22nd, 2016, at 5:30 am, I boarded the Amtrak Train to New York City, a three hour ride on the train, and it was crowded. It was a very scenic view through the states of Delaware, New Jersey, and New York City. The train was traveling at a speed limit to which I was thankful for. Two hours into the ride, I needed to use the bathroom. I went to the bathroom, closed the door, and thought it was locked. I took my pants down and had now been in a squat position, only to have a man open the door without knocking first. Oops! Here I was, exposed to him and passengers closest to the bathroom, and for a moment I felt as though I was in the hospital again, stripped of my dignity, like a show and tell for all. We were both embarrassed, but he was very apologetic. Even when we got off the train, he was still apologizing. I laughed out loud and kept going. *Shit happens,* I thought.

When I got to NYC I had to catch another train to Lindenhurst, Long Island. To my surprise, the train ride did not negatively affect me. I tolerated it beautifully. When I got to the train station, I was met by my friend Candida, who was very happy to see me. She commented on how much weight I lost but also complimented me on how great I looked and how much my hair had grown. She then drove me to her house where I was greeted and warmly welcomed by her kids, husband, and brother in law. They were all happy to see me. I received so many hugs and kisses that it brought tears of joy to my eyes. They have always treated me as part of their family. Her kids are like my own, and my son Kyle has always been treated as one of her kids as well.

On Christmas day, December 2016, we all gathered around the dining table, full of all kinds of foods, deserts, and drinks. Of course, I took it upon myself and became the entertainment after a glass of wine. Maybe it was the altered me. I was not sure if I was permitted by my doctors to drink alcohol, but I had that glass of wine, and began to sing a Christmas Calypso called "Drink Ah Rum," by Scrunter. My instruments for the music included my empty wine glass and a spoon.

I knocked the spoon on the glass, got some rhythm, and had music. Of course I was dancing to my own music. But Candida did not leave me hanging. She joined in, and began to sing and dance with me and it soon became a party atmosphere. Her brother in law and her husband were very encouraging as well, and joined in. It was so much fun and I had the most amazing time, it sure did relax me. *This was exactly what the doctor ordered,* I kept telling myself. Candida and her daughter Emily drove me back to Maryland on December 27th, 2016. I was scheduled to return to work on the first of February, 2017.

January 8th 2017, it was 6:00 pm, and time to go to the aneurysm support group meeting, I did promise Dr. Armonda I would attend. As I arrived, Dr. Armonda and Lisa, his patient care coordinator, were glad to see me and warmly welcomed me to the meeting. I sat with the group and was surprised to see so many people that had experiences similar to my own. Before this happened to me, I had not heard much about aneurysms, nor had I cared for anyone who suffered a ruptured one. I listened to the others tell their story, and I no longer felt that I was in isolation. *Others had gone through this, I was not alone,* I said to myself. Then it was my turn to tell my story and how I dealt with it. I used a sense of humor when telling my story to sort of break the ice. They warmly received me. I learned so much from each and every one, how each of us handled it differently in our own way. Many of them had some deficits, and were experiencing some complications, but none gave up hope, all kept the faith, and we all were there to support each other. It was so nice to see. I was so glad I attended. The group meets once, every other month. I continued to attend when I could until leaving Maryland for Florida. The group is definitely needed for us. It has helped a lot of us that have attended.

During the month of January, when the weather permitted, I drove myself to the Buddy Allen Park in Greenbelt, and would take long, slow walks around the lake. At times I would sit by the lake and enjoy the song of the birds chirping, the ducks and swans in the lake, and tried to soak up the beauty of the nature that surrounded me. It was so peaceful. I was not truly a walker, had been a runner most of my life, but I had been limited for medical reasons. I was not sure if my body at this point could tolerate running, but was sure tempted to see. One day, I decided I would give running a try. Around the lake was one mile long. So I did, I ran around the lake pacing myself for one mile and felt good, no distress. I was so excited I called my friend Robert and shouted in his ear.

"I did it, I did it, I did it, Robert, I ran a mile!" I said. Now this was only one mile. I was a marathoner, ran three full marathons of 26.2 miles each and about fifteen half marathons of 13.1 miles each up to age fifty. But from my excitement of completing this one mile, one would have thought I had just completed a full marathon. It was such an accomplishment for me after having two major neurosurgical procedures, and the fact that I could run a mile without distress was such a blessing.

Chapter 8

Returning to Work

I continued to do a little bit more each day while on FMLA, this included dancing of course, until it was time to return to work. Feb 1st 2017, I returned to work, highly functional, but careful. After the first twelve hour work shift, I got home feeling extremely exhausted. I did not have to return to work the next day, not until the following day. When I got to work the following day, I sat with my director to discuss my work schedule. Sonia, the manager, was there after my first surgery. She was very understanding and empathetic and worked with me to give me the right schedule to fit my needs. She was no longer an employee there; therefore another person did the scheduling. I emailed this person, asking her to schedule me to work every other day like Sonia did, and not two consecutive days, as I wanted to give my body a rest in between those long twelve hour shifts. She informed me that she would try. My co-workers were willing to be shifted to accommodate my needs however, she did not speak with them, and instead she did exactly the opposite of what I asked. When the next schedule came out, she had me working two consecutive days each week. I met with her to discuss this schedule, and said to her that I felt she was setting me up to call out and to be fired, because if I call out too many times, I would be.

"I tried but this is the best I can do," She replied. The first week I called in sick on one of the two consecutive days that I was scheduled to work, but the second week I gave it a try. I was scheduled to work Wednesday and Thursday. I came to work Wednesday, had a very busy and rough day, and then returned on Thursday only to find out that three nurses called in sick. We would be working short, giving me seven patients to care for that day on a very busy and hectic floor. I immediately regretted coming in to work that day. I approached the director and told her I couldn't do this, it was too much for me at this point. She informed me that she would assist and get help. Well, throughout the day I did not receive the aid promised. I love what I do and care deeply for all my patients; this was not their fault and decided to do the best I could for all of them. Before beginning, I prayed to God for his presence and help throughout the day.

At the end of the day I was so exhausted, and very anxious to leave. I just wanted to get home as soon as my relief came. When she came, I rushed her to take the reports from me so I could get home. I just needed to get home, my body was telling me. I eventually left work, got into my car, and drove myself home safely. When I got in my house, the first thing I did was drop my bag in the living room and ran to my bed. When I got to bed, my entire body began to shake violently and I was unable to stop it. My face began to twitch. It lasted one minute. I knew it had to be a seizure because I was so weak and tired when the shaking stopped, but was confused that I was having a conscious seizure, having not heard of it before. Not during nor after the first and second surgery while in recovery both at home and at the hospital, I had not had a seizure nor anything like this. The next day I was so weak I could hardly get out of bed or do much. I called my friend Theodora for help. She came by, brought me my meals, and stayed with me for a little bit as my son was at work. When Theodora left, I lay in bed with my thoughts, thinking of how my director could not have empathy or compassion for her staff. She was a nurse first, how could she be so cold? I am a great worker, I am functional, all I asked for was some understanding, and she did not have that. Then I began to ask myself, *Do I want to continue to work in such a stressful and challenging an environment? Especially one in which some of the leaders do not understand that although I am functional, I am still healing?* At that moment I decided I would quit. I did not have another job offer at this point, but I was going to go with a leap of faith and resign. I began to draft my resignation letter and would ask my son to type it when he got home that night. I drafted the letter at around 1:00 pm, and then decided to close my eyes and get some sleep. At 5:00 pm the house phone was ringing in the next room, it woke me up but I decided to let the answering machine take a message. The message was from Doctor's Community Hospital, the hospital that was five minutes from my home that I was trying for years to get a job at.

"This is Tiffany from the human resource department at Doctors Community Hospital, this message is for Rosalind. We received your application for a position in our observation unit and I will like to have an interview with you. Please give me a call," The message said.

Wow! Is this for real? I kept saying to myself. *Wow! The beauty of faith. God you are magnificent, you work at your own speed and time, what perfect timing!* I said to myself. Needless to say, I got on my cell phone and called her to schedule an interview.

I returned to work on Monday, after having the seizure, and went directly to human resources and handed in my resignation. I gave them two weeks' notice. The human resource director was willing to work with me. She offered me several options but at that point my mind was already made up and I declined her offers. Then I took a copy to my director, she took it, read it, and all she said was okay. After seeing her response, I knew I had done the right thing by resigning. I mentioned it to my co-workers and everyone was shocked and asked how could they let a good worker like me go without trying to work with me, especially when the unit was already short staffed. I told them there were some things I have no control over. What I know I have to do is to take care of my health, and I would not be good for my patients if I was not good for myself. My co-workers were worried about how I would pay my bills since I did not have a job to go to. I told them I was not worried. I am a damn good qualified nurse and I would find a job.

I set the job interview at Doctors Community for the day after I resigned from that hospital. I went to the interview scheduled for 10am that Friday in April 2017. I had the best interview ever, got home, laid in bed and was relaxing. At 2pm I received a call from the human resource department at Doctor's Community Hospital informing me that the Director of the Observation Unit loved the interview and wanted to offer me the job. *This was not happening, is this truly happening to me? I just could not believe this,* I said to myself. The Holy Spirit was sure working in my life. Needless to say I accepted the offer and was set to begin working on May 1st, 2017, at Doctor's Community Hospital, five minutes away from my home. How sweet was that? This also gave me two weeks to rest before beginning the new job. During the interview, I did inform the director that I would like to work every other day and not consecutive days. She informed me that it would not be a problem. I began to work and functioned beautifully, and this director was the sweetest person I have ever met. She was so calm, so understanding and a good leader. I loved working under her leadership.

Chapter 9

The Decision

What I have noticed after the surgeries is that during the winter months, when I am exposed to the cold, I begin to experience headaches; they are not typical headaches, but they feel like electrical sparks going off in my head, and I find myself feeling very nervous when driving in the snow. I had not experienced this before. Now I reviewed the voice that came to my head while vacationing in West Palm Beach in July 2016, which was saying to me that this will be my next destination. I thought this might be a good way to decrease my stress levels. I lived in a single family home with a very huge yard, which meant cutting lots of grass during the summer and shoveling snow during the winter, plus maintenance of this one thousand square foot home. I could not engage in any of those tasks now that I had the aneurysm. I discussed my leaving Maryland to Florida with my son Kyle and my friend Robert, and they all agreed that I should do what was best for me, and that they would support me with whatever decision I made. My neurologist also advised me to keep my stress levels at a minimum.

Okay. I was going to pack up and move to Florida. My search for homes began online; I was interested in condos only which would be less work and less maintenance, meaning no lawn and no snow. I saw a few that I liked which were located in West Palm Beach with a waterfront view. While searching, a realtor couple, Michelle and Steve Armowitz from Remax, saw my interest and began to correspond with me. Immediately a friendship between two strangers developed. I informed them that I had to sell my home in Maryland first before I could purchase in Florida. They volunteered to help me sell my home. Since they were not licensed in Maryland, they recommended an agent in Maryland who could represent me.

I got a good agent, a female, who worked with me on selling my home in Maryland. With that realtor we found two interested buyers who signed contracts, but unfortunately along the way both contracts fell through. I decided to change realtors. This time I asked Michelle and Steve to find me another good realtor, but a man this time. I was a bit aggressive when it came to things like this and did not find the female agent aggressive enough. They introduced me to Mr. Davis, another Remax agent and together we got my home sold within six weeks of working together. My home was put on the market at the end of April 2017, and was sold on September 7th, 2017. I now had to find a place to live for me and my son before moving to Florida. I would not leave for Florida until I had the angiogram, and was cleared by Dr. Armonda. I found an apartment in Greenbelt, even closer to the hospital. It was now taking me three minutes to get to work. I would live there until I was cleared and ready to move to Florida. While waiting, I would continue to work on getting the condo. I narrowed it down to three that I liked. From my first choice to my last choice, I saw it online and took a virtual tour of the unit. I had not gone in person to see it. After selecting these three, I went on to search for jobs in Florida. In the search engine, I typed in hospitals in West Palm Beach, and the first one that popped up was Good Samaritan. When I looked at the address, to my surprise it was located on the same street as the three condos I just selected. I sent my nephew, who once lived in West Palm, to check it out for me when he visited in early October. Nigel, my nephew, did look at all three one bedroom condos and got back to me with what he thought.

"Rosie your number one is the best one with a great view of the water. And the hospital you mentioned, Good Samaritan, is two blocks away," He said. This was music to my ears. I immediately called the realtors Michelle and Steve and told them to draw up a contract.

"Without seeing it in person?" They said to me. Yes, I trusted Nigel, plus the virtual tour gave me a thorough view of the apartment. I knew what I liked and this was it. And so we went into contract. The closing date was set for December 7th, 2017. Before closing, I decided to take a trip for my birthday at the end of October, my first and only time seeing it in person. It was beautiful with a great view of the intercostals and it did not disappoint me. The hospital was so close within walking distance of the condo. After returning to Maryland, I went on Good Samaritan's website to search for jobs. There were many vacant positions. I applied for an RN position for the Newbern Unit but was not expecting to get a response for a while. I was thinking perhaps after I relocate, but to my surprise within one week, around November 20th 2017, I received a call from the director of the unit asking me to come for an interview in two days, shockingly.

"I am still in Maryland, can we reschedule for Dec. 7th, I will be in Florida for the closing of my home," I said. *I can take care of both in one trip*, I thought. This is not bad. December 7th approached, and I was in Florida. My interview was scheduled for 11:30 am and closing at 1:00 pm. The interview went well; Michelle and Steve picked me up from the hospital and took me to closing. During closing, I received a call from the hospital human resources department asking me for a second interview. It could not be done that day, therefore we rescheduled for another two weeks because I would have to fly back and forth between Maryland and Florida. The second interview took place, they liked me for the job and I was offered the job. The pay was within my asking range so I accepted it.

Now my biggest task was to inform my current director at Doctors Hospital of my resignation. Oh this is going to be so difficult for me; she has been so kind, so understanding, and so full of compassion and empathy. I went to her office on December 9th, 2017 to hand in my resignation. I looked her in the eyes and could not find the words. Then I asked her if I could give her a hug, and we were in embrace. And as we were in embrace, the words came out and I handed her the letter of resignation. She took it, expressed her sadness, and told me it would be quite a loss for her hospital and she wished me all the best in my future endeavors. In three weeks I would be leaving for what would be my final destination. One more thing left to take care of before leaving Maryland for good and that was the angiogram. I could not make another move until I got the green light.

The angiogram was done on November 16th, 2017 and per Dr. Armonda and Dr. Lieu, everything looked good and was functioning well. There was no more aneurysm. Here was my green light to Florida. *Geez, is this a blessing or what? This is so surreal I can't believe it, someone pinch me I must be in a dream!* I thought to myself. But it was all happening. It was coming together and was meant to be. God had it all planned, I could not have planned this better myself. I do feel like I am living my second life, and I must say I like this life better than the first. I have become quite a different person. I am noticing many changes within myself, from the negative me to a now positive thinker, the now calmer me from the once quick tempered me. I am more forgiving, more active in fun filled activities, less work and more play, and best of all less stress.

Although this first appeared as a setback in my life, it turned out to be the total opposite. It was a set up for the great things that are happening to me today. Many changes had to be made, but all those changes turned out to be the best thing for me. The only thing that I am very confused about is that I am experiencing guilt. When I share my story with others, I often get back: well I know someone who had the same happened to them and they died, or they had a stroke, or other complications. I often feel so guilty when I hear this. I am not sure why I survived without deficit. I know that someday it will be made clearer to me as to why I was saved. The most I can do for others is to continue to educate them on living a healthy lifestyle. Soon after my first aneurysm and during my recovery period, my son left to go to his friend's birthday party. When he returned I asked him about the party. He told me a lot of his friend's family was there and he met all of them and he had a great time. One week later he was on his way to the same friend's house again and I asked how his family was doing. He informed me that the friend's cousin, who was just at the birthday party completely fine, two days later was riding his bike from work, fell off the bike, and died on the spot. The doctors said it was a ruptured brain aneurysm; he was only twenty eight years old. I could feel the pain and fear in his voice. My entire body at this point was so cold, and my eyes began to fill with tears. This boy just began his life and now he was gone and I was here. *Why am I here?* I kept asking myself, and the guilt returned. Then I asked Kyle to sit for a moment. I decided to make this a teaching moment.

"Kyle I am not sure why these things happen but what I do know is that we all have to take care of ourselves. We cannot control genetics and some things are beyond our control. But when we live a healthy lifestyle we lessen our chances of worst case scenarios. Per my doctor if I did not maintained a healthy lifestyle, one without drugs or alcohol or tobacco, I may not have survive the ruptured aneurysm. If you smoke and drink alcohol, you may want to think about quitting and you may want to start eating a healthier diet. I do not know if you will ever have the same happen to you, what I can tell you is that if you are having any related symptoms like headaches, dizziness, lightheadedness, or any symptoms, seek medical attention immediately and get a scan or MRI. Do not sit on it," I said to him.

I spent Christmas with my son and on the next day, December 26th, 2017, I packed my bags and headed for Florida. Robert and I left Virginia at midnight that night, and drove to West Palm. It was a long, fourteen hour drive, but we made it there safely. I once again surprised myself and did superbly well on the trip and, believe it or not, I did most of the driving. God performs miracles every day and I am living proof of one. My apartment is on the 9th floor of the penthouse with a spectacular view of the intercostals and the city of West Palm. The condo is in a gated community, so I feel very safe. I have made several friends within a few months of occupancy. I have been told by one of these friends to go to the Mandel Library in downtown West Palm Beach and I decided to check it out. This is no ordinary library. I have never seen a library this huge in my life. There are four floors, all stocked with videos, CDs, books and music of all genres. It was not so much the variety of these things that caught my attention, but them offering various types of classes and it was all free. They offered Zumba for both young and older adults, yoga, Argentine tango, Pilates, eccentrics, Tai Chi, and Hard Core workouts. It's amazing; on my days off from work I take Zumba, Tai Chi, yoga, and tango. Besides the library there is so much more to do and see in downtown West Palm Beach. Every Friday and Saturday night, there is a live music band at City Place and Clematis by the water on Thursday nights. I attend all three at times and dance the night away. It is so much fun. How could I not keep my stress levels down? This is the right place for me. I left Maryland to Florida with aim of reducing or eliminating my stress and I must say in Maryland my stress level on a scale of one to ten, it was one hundred. At this point in my life I would say it's now a zero to two.

Chapter 10

Memories of Childhood

I grew up in a time and a world that's a far cry to the one in which I live in today. If we could only turn back time to where morality, mannerism, values, unity, love for thy neighbor, and family values were emphasized, practiced, and cherished. It would make this world wonderful and be in much better shape. I was born and raised in a small remote village, Caparo, in the South Central region of Trinidad along the twin Island of Trinidad and Tobago, located in the Caribbean. Its population of twelve hundred people was made up of a very diverse group, deriving from various ethnicities, religions, and cultures. From East Indians, Chinese, Syrians, English, French, Spanish, and African heritages.

In this small village everyone knew each other and children were raised not only by their parents or family members, but by the villagers as well. Everyone looked out for each other. Respect of your elders was not a choice but a standard. My memories of childhood date back to age six. September 1968 was the beginning of my school year. I remember walking almost a mile to school, at times alone, and at times with the neighborhood kids. At that time of morning, almost all the elders sat in their front porches watching out for the kids on their way to school.

When passing your neighbors you had to greet them, every single one of them, with good morning or hello. If you didn't, it was not uncommon for them to discipline you right there and then, and inform your parents, and when you got home from school your parents would give you the second dose of discipline which at times was a slap on your hands or butt.

Seventy five percent of the population was entrepreneurs. Farming was a big part of the village. Most of the people in these villages were farmers including my father, and others were carpenters, seamstresses, food vendors, fishermen, and some shop owners. The villagers built the village using their individual skills. Bartering was quite common. It was common practice that my father would trade his crops such as yams, beans, coffee, oranges, mangoes and his chickens and ducks for beef, pork, or goat with his neighbors, who had animals but did not plant based food. We very seldom shopped and or paid for food outside of our community. I would sit on the front porch of our home and see the Syrian man coming down our street with his bag full of beautiful fabric, from silk, to cotton, to polyester, and I would call to my mother so she could select and purchase the best ones to make our dresses before the other neighbors got a chance to. Then there was the fisherman driving his pickup truck full of freshly caught fish.

"Fish, fish, come and get your fish, we have salmon, kingfish and snapper," He would chant, and the villagers would come running with their pans to purchase the fresh fish. I so enjoyed those moments.

My parent's home sits in the middle of a richly cultural, ethnic, and religiously diverse group of people. The neighbor to the left and right of our home were East Indians and Hindus. Directly opposite us were East Indians Muslims, to their left and right were some Chinese and Spanish whose religions included Catholic and some Baptist. What I enjoyed most growing up in this very diverse community was participating in the vastly rich, cultural celebrations. In T&T, national holidays are given to the various religious groups to celebrate their religious occasions and holidays like Diwali, the Hindus festivals of lights which usually falls between September and October, or Ramadan for the Muslims, a religious holiday of fasting and prayers, and Christmas.

On these festive religious days such as Diwali, they would prepare their Indian delicacies and package them, then distribute them to their non Hindu neighbors in the morning and in the evening of the holiday. They usually participated in Puja, a ritual of prayer and feast with their customs on display, and the entire village was invited. My sisters and I, during our teenage years, often attended. We would sit on the floor with them and eat their traditional vegetarian food on banana leaves with our hands after the prayer services were performed by the pundit, their religious leader. I so enjoyed this practice. Then they would light their Diya's and display them on bamboo arrangements and put on a big show for the neighbors with the beat of the Indian drums and dances performed by Indian dancers in which everyone participated. This practice was evident in all groups, on their specific religious celebrations.

At this early age growing up in such diversity, I learned early that although we might look different, speak in different languages, and worship differently, we are all created equal and can live in racial harmony; instead of fighting each other we enjoyed, appreciated, and celebrated each other differences, and that's what I grew up seeing in my village. What is so great about this is that we did not have to travel the world to get a taste of different food or enjoy different cultures or expand our horizon, we did it right at home. We slept with our doors open; neighbors walked in at any time and were always welcome. Children played freely outside of their homes and in the streets without fear. "It takes a village to raise a kid." This was so evident in the village in which I was raised. I am who I am today because of my upbringing by all my neighbors and my parents.

Born the seventh child of my parents Theodore and Irene Brewster, I lived in a tiny wooden two bedroom home with my seven sisters until age twelve when we moved into a bigger house, built by the entire family with my father in the lead. I never met my brother; the only boy from my parents who I learned was born just before me but lived only to be nine months and died from gastroenteritis. Sleeping was quite a challenge for us girls in a one bedroom, with a full size bed for eight girls. If you did not make it in time to secure your space on the bed when night fell, you had to sleep on the hard floors. At times, up to six of us slept in the bed, three in the horizontal positions and the other three in the opposite direction.

My father was a self taught carpenter and a farmer who worked intermittently due to severe chronic asthma. My mother was a homemaker. We had no electricity, night light came from candles and lanterns, and we had no running water. My father would catch the rain water via spouts into barrels, and when there was no rain, we would walk a mile to the well to fetch water in buckets that were placed on our heads. We had no stove, but an open fire surrounded by bricks, filled with sticks, and coal pots were used for cooking. My mother would make the best bread and food from that fire. Needless to say, we lived in poverty. But one would never know, and honestly it did not occur to me because I was very happy growing up. There was constant laughter, play, love, and joy. We were never left hungry, always fed. I remember when I was around age fourteen, coming home from school one day, my mother was not home to cook, but my father was and all he found was rice and some eggs, so he prepared that for us. There were not many eggs to go around, but he divided it for us and was left without for himself.

"I never heard of rice and egg before," My sister complained. I was happy to have something to eat. Then I looked at my father's plate and all that was left was about two spoons of rice. He did not take any eggs for himself. I watched him then sprinkle some brown sugar over the rice and ate that as his meal. He left himself out, but made sure we ate. It's only later on in life when I became a parent I realized that is what most parents do. They leave themselves out and take care of their kids first. Fortunately for us, my father inherited about an acre of land in which our tiny wooden house sits on, and many acres of farmland three miles away which earned him a living. However, he was smart enough to plant fruit trees and food crops along the side of the property in which we lived, and it was used as the fencing that separated his property from the neighbors. These fruits trees and food crops served as our meals.

I remember looking forward to the break of dawn to begin climbing some of the fruit trees with my sisters. We would begin with the trees in front like the tangerines, mangoes, plums, and bananas, and worked our way to the ones in the back. By the time we got to the back, we were so full, and it was time to go to school. The Caparo Roman Catholic School I attended was located 0.8 miles from my home. Therefore we walked to school, but many a times my younger two sisters and I would walk to school barefooted, because my parents could not afford shoes for all eight girls. We had to wait until my elder sisters could no longer fit in theirs, then it was handed down to the next in line. Thank God the school required uniform which made it easier for my parents. My mom would buy the material and sew our uniforms so we each had a few uniforms and did not have to worry about what to wear to school.

Since my father had no boys and no money to pay anyone to work the farmland, we his girls, and my mother, together with him, worked the farmland to earn a living. He produced many crops such as coffee, cocoa, cashew nuts, and oranges which he sold to the Trinidad and Tobago Agricultural Department for export.

At age ten after coming home from school and finishing my meal, it was time to get dressed in our garden clothing and grab the produce bags and walk three miles behind my father, who rode his bike, to the land to pick the coffee, cocoa, cashews, and many other crops off the trees. We bagged them, placed the bags on our heads, and walked back another three miles to home. Many of times, we fussed and complained, but those fell on deaf ears.

"Hard work brings great reward, it toughens you, you will be stronger than you can ever imagine," my father would often say. This went on until my teenage years when I graduated from high school and landed myself a government job, and earned somewhat of my freedom at least from working the land every day to some weekends.

My father was a very tough guy whom I looked up to. He was my hero, and mentor. At times when he would have an asthma attack, he would be so sick, and I would stand outside his bedroom door and peep through the cracks of the door to see him struggling to breathe. At times, I thought it was the last breath he would take; it looked to be so bad, and I was so sad and scared that I could not help him much. Then after a few hours of his inhaler and herbal medicine and rest, he would bounce right back and be ready to go. One day he looked so worried, I did not know what was happening, until I asked my mother what was wrong. She informed me that some of the neighbors were fighting him for land space which was his and he may have to go to court, plus he wanted to build a bigger house, but was struggling financially. The challenges were beginning to take a toll on him, however, he was not one to quit. Then one day, one of his friends whom he confided with told him about a person he should see that could help him. This person was called a see-a-mon or a fortune teller; however he was very spiritual, some would say a prophet. Mr. John was that prophet and his friend swore he was very good and would be helpful to us.

I was approaching ten and a half years of age, and was about to take my common entrance exam and if I passed it I would be given free secondary education, the first to do so in my family. My sisters before me did not have this opportunity. The eldest girls ranging in ages eighteen to twenty two had already left home, and were working and living in the city. At this age, one day my father gathered my two younger sisters and me and took us with him to see Mr. John who lived five miles away in another village. When we got there he greeted us and asked my father to send us in one at a time. My two younger sisters went before me, and when they came out they were shaking and crying, I did not know what happened in there. I was reluctant to go in the first place because I did not believe in this. My thoughts then were, if you believe in it, it will hurt. Then it was my turn to go in. Seeing the effects it had on my two sisters, my father decided he would go with me. I was not scared. The room was very dark, except for some candles and a make shift altar with a Jesus on the cross. We sat down across the table opposite Mr. John. He took my hands, closed his eyes and began to mumble something, and then he opened his eyes and looked at me. I looked him directly in his eyes and did not blink but I was not afraid and I believed he could tell that I was not scared.

"This one is special," He said to my father.

"They all are special," My father replied.

"No this one is different; there is something quite different about this one. This one would bring about many changes, changes you would not imagine, and the changes will be happening soon," Mr. John said. I had no idea what he was talking about, and did not think that I was any different from my other two sisters. Then he give my father many different verses in the Bible to read and told him what type of spiritual sacrifices he would have to make to overcome the negative, (evil), things that were happening in his life. When we came outside, my sisters were surprised to see that I was not crying. I remember saying to them why should I cry, he is just another man, and I am not scared of him.

A few months later, I sat and passed my exam and was on my way to free secondary education. During my junior years at secondary school I was a quiet kid. I did not talk much, had long thick black hair that my mother would comb into two long braids, and the kids on the bus and at school would tease me. They called me all type of ugly names, and they attempted to bully me. I ignored the words, but when they tried to physically hurt me I would fight back, and later when they found out that I could not be bullied, they stopped. Shortly after attending secondary school my father began to get many calls to build houses and his produce was now bringing in better profits. In all honesty things were getting better for us. I became the first to do everything, the first to go to free secondary school, to get my driver's license, to land a government job, to migrate, to go to college, and to own a home. Was this a coincidence or was it truly prophesized, I could not say at that time. Mr. John had been dead for more than forty years but after my experience with my aneurysm on that faithful day, Mr. John surfaced in my memory and now I was beginning to believe that in my entire life thus far, there were divine and spiritual interventions that I did not recognize, which were leading me to my destination.

Growing up was not just about hard work, I had a lot of fun as well. We as a family prayed together, ate together, played, together and danced together. I looked forward to weekends when the entire family would gather after the work was done, have meals then play cricket, soccer, fly kites, or pitch marbles. Some of the kids in the neighborhood would come over to my house and we would play until dusk. My father was often the referee in these games. The games were loud, full of laughter, and excitement. After the games on Saturday night, my father would turn on the small radio and we would listen and dance to the music. I often would dance with my father; he was not as great of a dancer as my uncles but he sure was able to move me across the room. Dancing was very much a part of my life growing up. It occurred quite often at my house, but excessively during the long Christmas holidays when my uncles would be paranging, moving from home to home with their musical instruments and Latin songs and dance. My grandmother was born and raised in Venezuela, but moved to Trinidad as a teenager and married my grandfather. So we got the Latin blood from my grandmother. They would come to our house last, and by then they were intoxicated, half of them vomiting all over the place and we the kids then had to clean it up. Then they would drag us to dance with them. I remember at times when we knew they were coming, my younger sister and I would run and hide under the bed. But we did not stay there for long because they found us, dragged us out, and danced with us. This was fun at times when they were not drunk because I would not have to smell their alcoholic breath. This is how I learned to dance by dancing with my drunken uncles. Every year on Boxing Day, the day after Christmas, which is also a holiday in Trinidad, my father would keep a party under our house. It was the biggest party held in the neighborhood yearly, as everyone was welcome and food and drinks were always in abundance. A variety of music was played by the DJ from calypso, to Spanish music, to Reggae, and some Indian music. Everyone in the neighborhood and nearby villages looked forward to coming to the Brewster's party yearly.

I developed a better relationship with my father than I did with my mother. I admired that my father was strong and brave and so independent. He never turned down his girls. He was always there for me. I remember when it was time for me to graduate from junior high and our parents had to attend, I asked my mother and she turned me down. She made a pretty pink dress for me but would not go with me. It was my father that went with me. He did not just attend the ceremony but stayed with me for the dance. So my date at age fourteen at my graduation was my father, and he danced with me too. When I had my son and it was time for his Christening, I invited both my mother and my father, and again my mother turned me down, but my father came from Trinidad in the middle of April. That year it snowed and it was his first time experiencing such cold temperatures. But he stayed for about two weeks and helped me with Kyle, his grandson. This was his second visit to me in the U.S. The first time he came during the summer. A few years later when talking to him I asked him when he was coming back to the states to see me.

"Girl I am still cold from that snow, so I can't say if I will be back," He replied. But he was always fun to listen to.

My mother on the other hand is sweet in her own ways, a good woman, and did what she knew how to do, but she is very timid and while growing up and watching her I found her to be very dependant and in some ways weak. However, she is very giving of herself and was always the peace maker and kind towards others. All I truly wanted from her was for her to find her independence and to be stronger and braver like my father. When I began to work in the government of T & T, every six months I would work in a different ministry. I was in a position at the ministry of works where I was a recruiter, recruiting men and women for projects like building pavements and cleaning roads. Being in this position I saw an opportunity to give my mother the independence she so deserved. My father was the one who helped me get this position, so I ran the idea by him and surprisingly he agreed it was a good idea. I asked my mother if she would give it a try and she agreed to, and so I gave my mother her first job, and boy did I see changes in her. She began to glow. She made a lot of new friends including men as she was now surrounded by them, whom also found her attractive and her attitude changed. She became a different woman and happier as she now had her own paycheck. She worked for quite a while after that and became more of an extrovert than she ever was.

Now, one would think that a family like mines that did so much together would forever be that way: unified, giving, selfless, but as time changes, so do people. Now that everyone has grown and have lives and families of their own, things have changed significantly between the siblings. Many have become self-centered and have allowed greed to come between their relationships with each other. This greed has lead to fighting for the property we all once lived in together that was owned by my father who has since passed away. Instead of wanting to keep it as a family property in which we can come together and host family gatherings the way it used to be, instead a couple of the siblings are seeking sole ownership which has brought a huge division in this once unified family.

Family

"When they wrong you, you speak up, fight
for what you believe in if you have to
When you are in the wrong you put your tail
between your legs, surrender, own up to it apologize
if you have too, be the bigger person.
Be strong, know who you are, believe in yourself, keep the faith,
Fear no man, but God." (My father)

My father- AKA- "The Lone Ranger" AKA- "Police." Gone but not forgotten. The man I most admired, a fearless, courageous, brave, strategic, hardworking fierce leader. He wore a very tough exterior but inside was a gentle, kind, generous soul.

Chapter 11

Memories of Childhood part 2

"Rosie," he calls me. "Get your typewriter and come type this letter for me," Said my father. I was only twelve years old at this time and just began junior secondary school. My father asked his sister, my aunt Rita who lived in Boston at the time, to send me a typewriter and teaching material on how to type. I taught myself to type by my father's urging. I sat as he told me to and began to type this letter.

"Dear Mr. Attorney General, there is a narrow drain and an ineffective culvert which passes through my property and it is in dire need of repair or replacement. Each time it rains heavily it floods the entire neighborhood, shutting down the village. Roads become impassable; no one can get in or out. It affects me the most. I get five to six feet of water under my house, trapping us for days upstairs, unable to get downstairs. It affects all crops and animals as well. Mr. Attorney General I have brought this to the attention of my local government and they informed me that money was allocated for this project; however it was never used for this project, instead through my own investigation I learned it was taken by the County Council members for their own personal use. This is a serious problem and it is negatively affecting the villagers. I would like for you to look into this matter," He stated. And so the letter was mailed to the Attorney General's office. I did not know my father had such intelligence, all he had was up to a third grade level of education. *How could he write such a good letter?* I thought to myself.

From that day, whether I liked it or not, I became my father's personal secretary. When his carpentry/builder contracting business began to boom, I was the one at the typewriter typing out the estimates to build houses for his clients. Unlike others, my father provided free estimates and as a result had many more clients which meant more work for me without pay. But I think he must be a genius because I was a very shy kid growing up, I did not talk much, so much so that I could not pronounce some words and could not articulate myself. By encouraging and at times forcing me to write, I was taught how to communicate and because of him doing this, I began to express myself through writing.

A couple months later my father received a letter from the Attorney General's office, stating that the matter was addressed and money was relocated for a new drain and culvert to be built. The drain had no name before but according to the letter from the attorney general's office. It was addressed as "Brewster's Drain." Now my father had a drain named after him. At this tender age I learned a valuable lesson from my father and that is to stand up and fight for what you believe in, especially when you believed you have been wrong, and not to be afraid to be an advocate for others as well as for yourself.

"Theodore, don't go to the land by yourself anymore, Mr. Kumar told me that some of the men, (our neighbors that were hunters), were planning to shoot you and make it look like an accident," My mother said.

"They better make sure I am dead when they try, because if I am not, they will be," My father responded. Did I mention that he was very stubborn too? My father was not a wealthy man but had a few enemies in the neighborhood who were jealous of his inheritance of a great amount of farmland, and another lot of land in which he himself later built a huge house on to shelter his large family. My father was a self taught carpenter, builder, and contractor. He later became a household name for building great houses throughout Trinidad and Tobago. He worked hard and made many sacrifices to take care of his family. Some of the neighbors who lived in closer proximity to our property fought him for land space, claiming it was theirs, but he fought them back in court and won, and for that they held grievances against him.

One day, despite my mother's warning, my father went to the farmland three miles away from our home all by himself to pick the produce. Thank God Mr. Kumar, who had his own farmland bordering ours and was a friend of my father, was there as well. The hunters who had planned to kill my father were there waiting for him, apparently having watched him leave the house, they followed him without him knowing. While my father worked the front part of the land, they went to the back, knowing that he would come to the back next. When he went to the back and was picking the coffee and cocoa off the trees, he heard a gunshot and dove to the ground. They fired at him, thankfully they missed, and before they could attempt again Mr. Kumar, himself a hunter, fired his gun and called out.

"Brewster are you alright? I will get them, stay down," Mr. Kumar said. It was then the two men ran away, but not before Mr. Kumar got a good look at them and was able to tell my father who they were. When my father got home, he told us what had happened. Of course my mother was furious with him for going by himself. The next day when my father left the house, he went directly to the two men home and confronted them with his machete in hand. I do not believe he went with intentions to kill, but to scare, and he succeeded. He scared the life out of them all. They never messed with him again.

Chapter 12

The Attempted Kidnapping

My third sister had a child at the age of 19. She was unmarried and broke up with the father of this child three months after giving birth. She was struggling, had no means of taking care of this child by herself, and therefore my parents took the child and raised her. I was only twelve at this time, and helped in raising my niece who became more of a sister than a niece. She had never met her father who lived three towns away, a forty-five minute drive. None of us dated anyone in our village; our relationships with boys were always long distance, mostly due to the fact that the boys in the neighborhood would not ask us out because of fear of my father. Therefore, no one knew who we dated, and in my sister's case no one knew who the father of my niece was.

There was this guy in the village that was always up to no good. He was unemployed, lived with his parents, and always got himself in trouble and would do just about anything for a buck. One day while I was walking to school, I saw this guy walking the streets naked. Only to find out he did this on a dare and for twenty dollars. Now at the age of seventeen, I had recently graduated from high school, was at home with no work or school at this time. On this day, it was just my father and I at home. My niece was around five to six years old and she was at school. She walked to and from school together with the neighborhood kids. It was around 2:00 pm and I was sitting on the front porch of our home and my father was downstairs taking a shower. While on the porch I saw this guy, the one that's always up to no good. He went to my neighbor's house opposite ours to meet his friend B, my neighbor. I could not hear what he said to B, but a few minutes later he came over on our property.

"I came to get my child," He said to me.

"What child, you know you have nothing here so you better get off of our property and stop your craziness," I said. Then he went back to his friend B, who told him that she must be in school.

"Let's go grab her there," He said. Now I did not know what this was all about, but I knew something was definitely wrong so I began to think quickly. I immediately ran downstairs and informed my father what just happened. My father ran out the shower naked upstairs to get some clothes, and said nothing to me. After some quick thinking I then told him I would run to the school and alert the teachers and principal, and stay with my niece until everything was under control. Knowing my father, I knew he would probably get himself into serious trouble if he caught up with these two guys, because he was very protective of his girls. My aunt lived about five houses down from us on the main street, and we lived on the side street. I ran to my aunt's house first and informed them of what was happening; my uncle and Lenny, my cousin, were home. I asked my uncle to help my father stop these guys and asked my cousin Lenny to meet my niece and I at the school to walk home with us after school was dismissed. My sprint training came in handy because after leaving my aunt's home, I sprinted to the school which was about a mile away. On my way, I passed the two men like lightening, knowing full well they would not catch me. I got to the school before they did, ran directly into the principal's office, informed him of the situation and asked him to hold dismissal of school until everything was under control. He immediately locked the school down, informed the school of a delayed dismissal, and sent me to my niece's classroom to inform her teacher and to stay with her.

After locking the school down, the principal himself went outside and found the two men standing outside the gate. He asked them to leave, but they did not. The guy that's always up to no good insisted he was waiting for his daughter. We did not have a police station in our village; the nearest one was about six miles away and getting a response took a while, therefore most situations were handled by the villagers themselves. Just when the principal turned his back to return inside the school, up came my father riding his bicycle with what was disguised as a cane in his hand but when you twisted the head off it was a very sharp sword that he obtained while serving in the British Army during World War II that he kept under his bed. It was his weapon of choice if and when needed. As he approached the two men, he twisted the head and pulled the sword out and when they saw this, they took off running. Before my father began his chase of them, he called out to the principal and asked if we were okay. Once he knew that we were there and safe he began to chase the guys. My father was so livid, he chased them for a couple of miles and did not stop until my uncle, who drove behind him, convinced him to give up the chase when the men ran into someone's home to seek refuge.

When the principal believed that the students were out of danger, he dismissed the school. Lenny my cousin was there when the school was dismissed and he walked my niece and I home, and stayed with us until my father got back. Later on, my father learned through his own investigation and the police investigation, the culprit that was behind this. After that day, he became more protective of us, especially his granddaughter who experienced this. The man in question never did step foot in our village again.

No charges were brought against my father. The man that was always up to no good never stepped foot on our street again, as a matter of fact it took him years before he came back to the village where his parents lived three houses down from my aunt's home. We were told that he went to live in the city. My niece Cathy did not know nor understood what was truly happening at the time, but was told later when she got older. She is now a fine very successful woman with a child of her own. To her, my father was her father, the only father she truly knew. But as she became a woman she had interest in finding her father. Having experienced this with her, and my role in the safe outcome of the situation, a special bond developed between us. This bond continues today even after migrating to the U.S. I would not say my father was a violent man, he was the opposite but if you messed with him or his children, there is no telling what he would do to protect himself or his family.

Chapter 13

Nursing

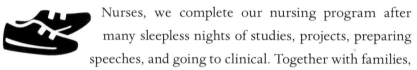 Nurses, we complete our nursing program after many sleepless nights of studies, projects, preparing speeches, and going to clinical. Together with families, many make the ultimate sacrifices necessary to become a Registered Nurse. You graduate from an accredited nursing program, now you are faced with the grueling task of sitting and passing your State's Nursing Board exam so you can be licensed to practice nursing in your state. You passed the Nursing Boards, you are now a Registered Nurse. You are excited, you are ready to go out there and save the world because you care and want to make a difference. You are happy to land your first job and reality begins to set in. "The real world" is here. Now you are left asking yourself, am I ready for the real world as a RN? In the classroom and throughout your nursing program you were prepared strictly by the classic text book standard, nothing or no one truly prepares you for the hospital or nursing home settings, "The Real World."

The hunt for jobs begins, it did not take you long to land your first RN job. Before you begin orientation on your new job, you begin to worry whether you will get the preceptor from hell because you have heard so many horror stories of preceptors. You are hoping you don't, because how can you learn under hell. You soon realize you no longer have the security of your clinical instructor or professor, but you are on your own. You make it through three months of orientation with sweat and tears and you are now on your own. First day on your own as a RN in your new job, and you are given a full assignment of five, six, in some cases seven patients- the toughest assignment- and you feel as though you have just been thrown into a pack of wolves. The Phrase- "Nurses eat their young," you are discovering is not just a saying, but a fact. What do you do? You are struggling, you ask your fellow nurses for help, and they all tell you they are too busy to lend a hand, knowing full well that you are a brand new nurse. You have a nursing assistant who is nowhere to be found, and half of the work that should have been completed by them is incomplete.

You are now in a new world with so much coming at you all at once. You are hit with insults from some impatient, egotistical, and obnoxious doctors. You are verbally abused by some patients and their family members. You are running around like a chicken without a head during your twelve hour shift. You accepted the job with a title of RN, but at the end of the day you have taken the role of many titles. You become the doctor because after some doctors make their thirty second visit with the patient, and do not explain much to them, they then call you the nurse with all their medical questions and prognosis. You become the janitor, the exterminator, the psychologist, the electrician, the dietitian, and the list goes on. You are performing in all these roles under one salary, the RN's and license. Many a times you want to use the bathroom but can't, you have to hold it because you are being pulled in every direction and your patients come first. Next thing you know you end up with a UTI or prolapsed bladder because you held it too long. Many nurses go without having a thirty minute meal break during working hours. If you don't have a candy bar or a piece of fruit or drink on you that you can quickly digest when you are in the med room or pantry getting something for your patient, you will perhaps collapse of hunger and low blood sugar and will not survive your shift. Many nurses do collapse.

Although we may appear to be super humans with all that we do, we are only humans and are subject to make mistakes. Especially under the conditions in which we work, mostly being short staffed, and God forbid we make a serious mistake that can harm the patient. You are immediately thrown under the bus and left there by administrators, doctors, or colleagues to fend for yourselves and the RN license you worked so hard to obtain is now in jeopardy.

During your nursing program you learn about Florence Nightingale and other women pioneers in the field of nursing. How they fought to make nursing a recognizable and respectable profession, and how well they work together to serve their fellow men and women and the contributions they have made to their field of nursing around the world. As a nurse, many of us want to carry on the mission they started, but it has become so difficult to do so knowing that it is not a respected profession as it should be. It is difficult to provide excellent care when nurses are given a ration of six or seven patients to one nurse. As a result, nurses are being burnt out and leaving the field in vast numbers. As nurses, you register in some unions and at times your own unions to fight for better working conditions and better care for your patients. You take your concern all the way from your administrators to your politicians, and for the most part your voices and concerns falls on deaf ears, but you do not give up, you continue the fight with faith and hope that one day you will be heard and the concerns and problems would be addressed, because you are an avid advocate for patients and yourself.

The American Nurses Association defines nursing as "the protection, promotion and optimization of health and abilities, prevention of illness and injury, alleviation of suffering through the diagnosis and treatment of human responses and advocacy in healthcare for individuals, families, community and populations."

As a nurse you took an oath to care without causing harm, and to practice by this definition. However it is difficult to do so when one nurse has to care for six, seven, sometimes eight patients, some of whom are high acuity patients. This often time leads to injury to patients, especially falls and unintentional neglect, since a nurse cannot be in seven to eight rooms all at the same time. This is so unfortunate for all parties.

Nursing is a profession that is highly needed today. People around the world are sicker at a higher rate than they have been in years due to the prevalence of terminal diseases like cancer, and the increase cases of heart diseases, diabetes, and kidney diseases to name a few. The baby boomer nurses are also retiring and with the increased workload for new nurses, many are burnt out and are running from the profession in great numbers. Although we are in high demand, we are still highly disrespected and are not recognized as a profession. From the outside looking in, it appears to be a respected and well compensated field to be in, but it is not in my opinion. It is not until you are in it that you realize it is not. For all the work a nurse does on a daily basis, they are still not well compensated nor given the respect they deserve. The way I see it, to be in nursing for the long haul, you must love it and have a deep passion for it; you must truly love caring for others and have so much compassion. If you don't, it will be a struggle to survive in nursing as a career.

Despite the many challenges we as nurses face on a daily basis, there are many great moments and a bright side to nursing. I compare nursing to a team sport. In team sports when one person scores a goal or a touchdown, the entire team wins because all the players contributed to him getting that ball to the goal post. This is the same thing in nursing, to save a life each and every day it takes the entire team and this is where we work as a team and all become winners. I will share two moments that stood out for me which showed the brighter side of nursing and teamwork.

There was a young man in his late thirties who was transferred from the ICU to the med-surgical unit in which I worked. He spent a couple of months in the ICU, had a trach and was connected to a ventilator. The doctors said there was nothing more they could do for him and told the family to consider comfort care because he may not have long to live. We continued to care for him, but he was in a comatose stage and we did everything for him. Two nurses and an assistant would be in the room together when giving patient care. We would spend sometimes close to an hour cleaning him, turning and positioning him, giving him passive range of motion exercises so his extremities would not become too stiff. At times some members of the team who were religious would pray for him, talk to him, sit with him, and his family would come and spend long hours with him; until one day the doctors advised them to place him on hospice care. Just before being transferred to hospice, one day while another nurse and I were in the room with him, he opened his eyes and began to make sounds, attempting to talk even through his trach. He was motioning and attempting to pull out the trach and we immediately called the doctors. They all came by and were amazed to discover that this guy came back to life. He followed every command the doctors gave and after a while with the entire team in the room. They took him off the vent and placed an oxygen mask on him as well as a Passy Muir valve. This valve allowed him to speak. A few days later this trach was removed and with a few weeks of physical and occupational therapy, remarkably this patient was ready to be discharged to rehab to begin his life all over again. The day of the discharge came and the entire team of nurses, doctors, RTs, PTs, OTs, and even the management team were outside his hospital room door with balloons, cheering him on. We were all clapping and happy to celebrate the miracle that we perhaps had a hand in. He spent months in the hospital and did not leave with any bed sores. This was credited to great nursing care and teamwork. This was the moment I felt most proud to be a nurse.

The second moment was in the earlier part of my nursing where I worked on the med-surgical floor before branching off to other areas of nursing. One day while at work on the weekend, I walked into my patient's room during my round only to find him unresponsive and not breathing. The patient was in cardiac arrest and he was in his fifties. I began CPR and called a code blue and within a minute the code team was at the bedside. After about five minutes of continuous CPR, we found a pulse, but still no breathing. It was the weekend so there was less staff in the hospital. By the grace of God, one of the best surgeons was working that day and came to the code. The surgeon was known by the name of Butcher, given to him by the staff because of the huge mess he made during surgery. He would save your life, but the people around him would have the blood on their clothes to prove it.

"Get me the trach kit, intubation was unsuccessful. We do not have time to take him to the OR, I'm going to do a tracheotomy right now right here!" He said after discovering the problem was respiratory. And so, the room on the med-surgical floor just became the OR, and it was all hands on deck. He was able to successfully trach the patient and then the patient was immediately transferred to the ICU. During the procedure the nurses the respiratory therapist that was assisting, as well as those that were closely observing, all got significant amounts of blood on their uniforms. No one minded because we saved a life that day, and that was all that mattered as a team, which was well worth it.

A few weeks later I was at the nursing station documenting and a gentleman came by. At first, I did not recognize him until he told me who he was. Three men behind him brought boxes and boxes of pizzas, chicken wings, cakes, sodas, food to practically feed an entire nation.

"What's this?" I asked.

"I brought this for you all, I wanted to say thank you and tell you all how grateful I was for saving my life. I would not be here today to tell the world about this hospital and it's amazing staff. This is the best hospital, I don't care if anyone says otherwise. You are all great!" The patient said. The staff gathered, we took pictures with him, celebrated his recovery but he did not do this just for one day or just our unit. He did it for an entire week, feeding us, the ICU staff, and the respiratory and therapy departments.

Despite the many challenges, and some dark sides that we as nurses face on a daily basis, it's the great moments like those mentioned that keep you going forward with hope that each day the darkness will be less, and there will be more happy endings.

I still do believe that nursing is a rewarding profession, especially when you get to be a part of positive patient's outcomes. However it is sad to see that many medical institutions have shifted their emphasis somewhat from a nonprofit enterprise with focus on good patient outcomes to a business venture where the focus is now on the bottom line, money for profit. This, in my opinion, now takes precedent over the welfare of the patients and the nurses.

When asked what I wanted to be when I grew up, I did not know what I would say, perhaps just work and make money, that was my answer. In my adolescent and teenage years I found myself arguing a lot and would not stop until I was declared the winner of the argument and was a bit aggressive, but quick in my thinking. With that fact in mind, I at times thought of becoming a lawyer. I did not think of being a nurse because I did not believe I had the patience to be one. But an old blind man saw something in me that I did not see in myself at that age.

My mother, a Catholic, was a member of the Legion of Mary Group in our church. The group's mission was to build better communities by helping those in need in their community. As a member she did her part by going to different homes finding their needs and helping them according to their needs. One day she came home from one of her meetings and said to my other two younger sisters and myself that one of us have to go and help Mr. Gabriel after school. Mr. Gabriel lived two houses from us on the opposite side of the street. He had recently lost his wife and now lived alone. He was about seventy years old, blind, and had several pigs they cared for. Mr. Gabriel was a railroad engineer and lost his eyesight from an accident at work. My other two sisters refused to go, so I volunteered to help Mr. Gabriel even though I was terrified of animals.

I was eleven years old and each day after school I would complete my homework if I was not working the land with my parents, and then go to help my neighbor Mr. Gabriel. I would assist him with preparing his meals, helping with the dishes, laundry, grocery shopping, and accompanied him to the pig pen so he could take care of his pigs. I would not go into the pen but stand outside and watch as he fed the pigs. Although he was blind, he knew where everything was and got around fine. After completing the chores I would sit with him and talk for a while. He was so full of wisdom; I enjoyed hearing his stories and learned so much from him. I actually looked forward to going to help him each day. He was very good to me. At times when I was leaving, he would give me money as school allowance. I never got this from my parents because they did not have enough to give me, therefore I welcomed this. When I returned home I would show my two sisters the money and they became envious, and I would tease them because they refused to help in the first place.

I did this for a few years until Mr. Gabriel found a family that moved in to live with him.

"You have a very kind spirit, you are full of compassion, you truly care for others, and as young as you are you are very giving of yourself. You have the qualities to be in the caring profession, you must become a doctor or a nurse as you will do well in those fields. I have two daughters who are nurses in England. Let me know when you are ready and I will make arrangements to have you go to England to study medicine or nursing," He said to me one day. At that point I was still a teenager and did not know what I wanted to be. I just told him okay, and left it at that.

At age twenty four I migrated to the United States and lived in New York. I found a job working as a nanny caring for three girls. I cared for them for four years. It was during those years I realized that I had the patience to care for others. I returned to Trinidad to get my green card, eight months pregnant at the time. On my visit to my village, I went to say hello to Mr. Gabriel, only to find out that he had cancer and was in the terminal stage of the disease. When I got to his house I entered from the back and stayed in the kitchen. I knew he was in the bedroom and unable to get out of bed, but I was so afraid to get close to him, why, I did not know. The lady taking care of him informed him that I was there. He asked to see me. I made it to the bedroom door but remained there and spoke to him from the doorway. He asked me to give him a hug but I would not move, my feet felt so heavy and my heart was beating so fast. I was so scared to get closer to him. It was so sad to see him in this condition. After a while I found the courage to go closer and eventually give him a hug, also saying my goodbyes to him.

"Remember what I told you, you have what it takes, become a nurse or a doctor, you will be great and I will be watching and smiling down from heaven when you find out how great you are," He said to me while in his embrace. I believe he knew he did not have much time left, and I was terrified.

"Okay," I said to him, and left with my eyes filled of tears and shaken up.

I returned to the states one week later. Two weeks after returning, I learned of Mr. Gabriel's death. After giving birth to my son, I stayed home for a few months to care for him. While at home, I gave Mr. Gabriel's advice some thought and decided that I would give it a try. Before doing so, at this point all I had was my high school diploma from my country. I would have to get my GED if I were to pursue a nursing degree to do college courses. I accomplished all of this, and then took a nursing assistant course, and became certified to be a nursing assistant. *I will try nursing assistant first, if I liked it and was good at it, I would then continue to pursue the nursing degree,* I told myself. At this time I was living in Brooklyn New York.

When I decided to go back to work, I found a job as a home health aide, caring for the sick and mostly elderly at their homes. I did this for a few years, and enjoyed it. It was while doing this that I desired to become a RN. I bought my first home in Queens Village NY, and moved to Queens. I lived in this home with my then husband and son for five years. While living in Queens, I found a nursing assistant job at the Veterans Nursing Home in Stony Brook Long Island and then transferred to Stony Brook University Hospital. This job was a one hour drive from my home. I made that drive every day from 5:30 am and returned home at 4:00 pm. It was at Stony Brook University that I made the decision to dive into nursing with the constant encouragement from the nurses and staff at Stony Brook. I then registered to begin my nursing education at Medgar Evers College in Brooklyn NY. I began taking my prerequisite classes that would prepare me for entrance into the nursing program. It was four and a half years in my new home, my son just turn seven yrs old, and I was going through a divorce and had just put my house on the market for sale. This did not stop me but propelled me to push harder to get this degree that would perhaps be a blessing in the life of my son and myself.

I was in college full time and I was working full time. I would leave my house in queens at 5:30 am, make the long drive to Stony Brook to work, return home at around 3:30 at times 4:00 pm, get my son from home in Queens, and take him with me to college for my classes that began from 4:30 pm to 8:30 pm. I had to take him with me because his father refused to care for him while I was in school, even though he was at home. My son was in school all day, then had to accompany me to my classes because his father was too angry, selfish, and full of revenge to take care of him. With his focus on hurting me, he failed to see that he was only hurting his son. But I did not let that stop me. I informed the professors and they allowed my son in the classroom. And here he was, at seven years old, in college, and the professors would say he was their best student. He would sit in the back of the class, very quiet, doing his homework, or drawing, or playing with his toys and, no one would know he was there. With all going on in my life at this time I was achieving A's and B's in my classes. Even though I was working full time, I took full time courses, twelve credits per semester, and maintained a grade point average of 3.5 and above. I was super focused. I remember one day I was up at 2:00 am practicing my speech in the mirror for my speech class presentation later that day. I held on to my belief in God and trusted that he would see me through it and he did. I was so focused I did not have time to stop and think about whether it could be done or how difficult it was, I was just doing it. The sacrifice I was making throughout school, I did believe would certainly pay off heavily for my son and myself.

It came time for me to leave NY and move to Maryland with my son. I found myself another job as a Certified Nursing Assistant at a nursing home, again a long distance from where I lived. I continued taking classes at a nearby two year college until I obtained all the required classes needed to get me into the nursing program. After completing my prerequisite, I applied for the two year nursing program. At this time it was very difficult to get into the nursing program because they could only accommodate sixty students per program, per semester, and only the top sixty would be chosen. After applying, it took two weeks to get an acceptance letter. I waited, two weeks past, but I did not receive my letter. I went to the college to inquire, only to learn that I did not get accepted, and they would not tell me more than that. On my way out the door, very disappointed, I ran into a guy that was in my anatomy & physiology II class. I asked him if he received his letter of acceptance and he informed me that he did. When I asked what his GPA was, I was stunned to learn it was 3.2 and he got in, and mine was a 3.6. Now I was furious and devastated. It takes a lot for me to cry, but on my way home the tears were just dropping. I got home and began to pace the floor. I was thinking of all the sacrifices I made, all that I put my son through, to not get into the program.

What do I do now? I grew angrier by the minute, but I knew I couldn't lose control. I knew I was not one to quit and if this was what I truly wanted to do, I would find a way. I then let my faith take control. So I took a deep breath and decided that I would find other avenues. I had to find a plan B, and that would be to find another college that would accept me. But before I do so I am going to fight this. I got my pen and paper and began to write letters to the President of the College, the Board of Directors, and the President of the nursing program informing them that I had proof that a less qualified person than me got into the program while I was bypassed, and would like to know why. At the same time I was on the phone with another college and got an appointment to meet with that college. Before going to the appointment at the other college, I received a call from the college that did not accept me, asking me to come in to meet with the Dean of the program. When I got there and met with her, she first informed me that they made a mistake. My transfer credits were not recorded and therefore were not taken into consideration during the selection process. She apologized and gave me a letter of acceptance. This was such a relief. I accepted and began the nursing program. Two years later I graduated from an accredited nursing program, took the Maryland Nursing Board exam, passed it, and became a RN.

MY PEOPLE
LET'S BRING FAITH INTO OUR LIVES
By
ROSALIND NOREIGA

FAITH:

SHE IS POWERFUL, SHE IS STRONG, SHE IS COURAGEOUS. SHE COMES BEARING TRUST, BUT SHE DOES NOT WORK ALONE. FOR HER PRESENCE TO BE EFFECTIVE, SHE HAS HER SISTER'S HOPE AND PATIENCE. WITH ALL THREE WORKING TOGETHER, THEY ARE A FORCE TO BE RECKONED WITH. AS THERE IS NO DOUBT, BUT CONFIDENCE AS TO WHAT THEY CAN ACCOMPLISH. FAITH, WHAT A COMPANION TO HAVE. YOU CAN TAKE HER ANYWHERE WITH YOU AND KNOW THAT YOU WILL ALWAYS BE SURROUNDED BY POSITIVE ENERGY. WITHOUT HER PRESENCE YOU WILL BECOME LOST AND STAGNANT. SHE IS THE BELIEF THAT WHEN YOU ARE AT YOUR DARKEST HOUR, IF YOU HOLD ONTO HER, THINGS WILL GET BRIGHTER. SO MY PEOPLE, LETS KEEP FAITH IN YOUR LIVES, FOR SHE WILL NOT DISAPPOINT.

Chapter 14

Migration

Many people around the globe who live in faraway lands and small villages have always had great aspirations for advancement in their lives. To fulfill those aspirations, they seek opportunities that may not be available to them in their birth nation but in nations that have endless opportunities for growth and they take advantage of those opportunities. Most do so through the proper channels. I was one of those aspires reaching for the stars and did not think that I could achieve it from my little village. So I journeyed to the north to begin my ascension.

At age 24 I decided I had enough of Trinidad and it was time for me to explore the world. I chose the U.S. first to migrate to. This decision was based on the fact that my Aunt Rita lived in Boston, the only person I knew lived abroad, and she and I had a good relationship. I had a great paying job working as an administrative clerk in the Trinidad and Tobago Government. I lived rent free at my parents house and had no bills, but this was not enough for me. I was not sure what I was in search of, I just knew I felt stagnant and wanted to go a lot further than where I were at the time.

I called my aunt Rita, informed her of my intentions, asked if I could move to Boston to work and live with her. She suggested New York instead of Boston, as it would be easier to find a job that would sponsor me to obtain legal status in the country. But I did not know anyone in NY, I said, only to find out from her that I had a cousin, my father's niece, living in NY.

"Your cousin Cheryl lives in NY, I will give her a call and ask her if she can accommodate and assist you on your quest, I will also give you her phone number so you can speak to her," she said. I had never met this person and my father did not tell me about her and later I learned that she lived with her father and did not keep in touch with her mother's side of the family. Therefore he did not know her whereabouts. I spoke to Cheryl again and we talked on the phone for quite a while. She then agreed that I could come and she would help as much as she could. Now that I had a place to stay, I could continue with my plans.

Fortunately for me, at the time I was acting secretary to the Chief Immigration Officer of Trinidad and Tobago Immigration Department. I informed him of my decision. He offered to help me get my visa to the U.S. by writing a letter to the U.S. Consulate of the U.S. embassy in Trinidad on my behalf. I then applied for a visitor's visa, and was given a six month visa to the U.S. Now it was time to inform my parents of my decision and seek their help financially to make the journey. Although I had no rent, nor bills to pay, money did not stay in my possession. I am a huge giver, a big spender, and not one to save. I had some money but needed a bit more as added security while in the U.S. being unsure how long it would take me to get a job. I went to my father, told him my plans, and asked for his help financially. My father did not hesitate, he took all the money he had in the bank, one thousand dollars, and gave it to me. My father and I had a different and special relationship. He believed in me. I then went to my mother and asked for her help. My mother was a very timid person and would let others make decisions for her. When I asked her for her help financially, my sister was next to her. Before she could answer, my sister told her not to give me any because she would be wasting her money and that I did not know what I wanted.

"She jumps from job to job, she is not serious, she is just going there to have a good time, she will be back without achieving anything," My sister said. With that said, my mother said no to my request. But little did my sister know that years from this day I would be the one offering to help her get her permanent visa to the U.S. as I am one not to hold a grudge.

I bought my ticket to the U.S. and was set to leave the land of my birth on May 28th, 1987. The week before I was to leave, my father had two friends over, two men of Indian decent and their custom was arranged marriages. My father told them of my plans.

"Brews why don't you get a nice Indian boy to marry your daughter and take care of her and not have her go to a strange big country all by herself," One of the men, Mr. Sugrim, said to him. My father laughed out loud.

"I have eight daughters and if there is one I am not worried about it would be this one. She is very independent, very strong, can take care of herself, she makes her own decisions, and I can't tell her what to do. I believe she will make it, because when she sets her mind on something, she follows through. She will be fine, and if I must say so myself, she is a younger version of me, I am not worried," My father said. Upon hearing this, it gave my confidence a major boost and for the first time, I was hearing my father believed in me. *I must then believe in myself,* I thought.

It was 6:30 am on May 28th, 1987 and I was saying goodbye to my family. I would be boarding the 8:30 am Pan American last flight in service out of Trinidad to the U.S. I went to say goodbye to my father.

"Go get them tiger, you will make it, as long as you are a hard worker, and have an English tongue in your mouth you can make it anywhere in this world; just use it and the tools given to you by us, and you will be fine," He whispered in my ear.

On the other hand my mother said something totally different that stuck with me for a very long time. She did not say have a safe trip, she did not say take care of yourself, nor that she would miss me or that she loved me.

"When you are sending money, send it by money order," She said.

This is the same mother who refused to help me financially when I was seeking her help. I boarded the plane and throughout the flight all I could think of was the last words spoken to me by my mother, and I was asking myself, *Who is this woman? Why is she being so cold? She does not believe in me or supports me like my father did.* However it was those words and the refusal to believe in me that made me more determined to prove them wrong and to prove to myself that I could and would make it. Here I was on my way to a strange place, a stranger to my new home with only three hundred dollars in my possession and an uncertainty as to when I would find work to support myself. Here I was taking a big leap of faith, but in my head all I heard was, *I will find a job soon, it's a land of many opportunities. I will find someone to sponsor me so I can work and live legally in this country. I will keep this positive attitude,* I told myself.

I got to JFK airport in NY that evening and was warmly greeted by my cousin Cheryl, who I was meeting for the first time. She took me to her apartment in Brooklyn. She lived alone in a small basement apartment. New environment, new country. I was excited to be here and knew I had so much to discover. Cheryl worked but took the weekends off to get me acquainted with my new environment, and since she worked I would have to travel to find work on my own. However, she did take the time to teach me about riding the railroads, the subways, and the buses. I had to learn how to get around Brooklyn and other parts of NY fast. My first cultural shock was that most people in NY got around by wearing sneakers even when going to work at businesses. I was used to wearing heels each time I left my home, but now I had to give up my heels for comfortable sneakers if I was going to run to catch trains and buses. It was quite interesting to see. I found NY to be quite a hustle and bustle, fast paced. I rode the subway and buses with her all weekend long and enjoyed it. We talked a lot, getting to know each other. She was fun to be with. During that weekend, we were also searching for jobs through agencies. We found a few agencies that I checked out on my own the next Monday.

On Monday June 1st, 1987 I set out to find a job. Cheryl gave me directions to the agency and told me what bus and subway train to take. I was not afraid, I viewed this as an adventure and was ready to take it on, remembering what my father told me, use the English tongue, so when I got lost, and could not find my way back, I did just that and asked for help. I got to the agency and was given a few job interviews, but they were all in Long Island NY. It was a long way from Brooklyn, even by train. I went to one on Friday June 5th, 1987 in Roslyn Harbor Long Island, NY. The woman who interviewed me at her home was looking for someone to care for her young daughter, five years old. The child and her spoke both Spanish and English, however her mother also lived with her and spoke only Spanish. She could not offer me the job because she wanted someone who was bilingual.

"I am sorry I can't hire you, but I have a friend who is looking for someone to care for her kids and I believe she will hire you, let me call her," She stated, and she did, and the friend came over to her house to meet me.

The friend and her two beautiful daughters met me at this person's house. My first impression of them was that they were not only beautiful looking, but kind, warm, and friendly. She invited me to her house which was about half a mile away from where we were, for an interview with her family. We pulled up in a long circular driveway to a huge mansion sitting on a hill overlooking the harbor, surrounded by a tennis court, a pool, a pool house, a jacuzzi, and a beautiful landscape. I had never been to such a huge home before. It was a historic house that I later learned was once used by pirates of the 19th century to store their stolen goods. There was a tunnel that took you from the harbor to the basement. Since it had turned into a private residence now, it had since been closed. We went inside the home. It had twenty five rooms and three floors. The top floor was their offices. They owned a sales associates business, and her husband was a top sales representative for companies like Nintendo, Atari, Apple, and Microsoft to name a few. She introduced me to her husband and her eldest daughter. They were a Jewish family. They all were friendly and warmly welcomed me to their home. The youngest child immediately attached herself to me. She grabbed my hand and held it throughout the time her mother was showing me around the home. The home was magnificently and meticulously kept. When we got to the third floor where the offices were, at the end of the floor were two huge guest rooms. We got into the one with the better view of the harbor and the youngest daughter, who was still holding on to me, looked at me.

"This is your room," She said. I had only met these strangers for about thirty minutes and somehow I felt as though I belonged here. *I was getting so much positive energy that there was no way I was going to turn this down if it was offered to me*, I was thinking. After touring the house, we sat and talked about the job and continued the interview. The job was to care for the three kids. They travelled a lot on business and were away from the kids for days at a time, especially during the electronic conferences that took place three times a year in different states. They were looking for someone they could trust with the kids, and one the kids felt comfortable with. She had a housekeeping crew that cleaned the house and they also had a butler from Barbados that did everything else. My focus would be the kids. She offered to sponsor me so I could get my work permit and later my green card. She also recommended a lawyer and offered to assist with the lawyer fees, but it was a contract, and I would have to stay with them until I obtained my green card. I would live in their house during the week, and have the weekends off. The salary offered was great for what I would be doing and getting in return. At the end of the interview they offered me the job. I accepted and would begin work on Monday June 12th, 1987. Her daughters were very happy. They drove me back to the train station. When I got back to Brooklyn and informed my cousin, she could not believe it.

"This was waiting for you Roz, you are only here one week and you already found a job, this is meant to be, you are so lucky," She said.

"I moved by faith, and this was all faith," I replied.

June 12th was here and I was on my first job in a brand new country. I began to care for my three girls. Yes! They became my girls. I spent so much time with them. I worked and lived there from Monday to Friday and lived with my cousin on weekends. Some weekends, mostly in the summer time, they might ask me to work when they were entertaining guests, and I did. These strangers became my family. They welcomed and trusted me, a stranger, into their house and treated me like family. I took good care of the girls, I treated them as though they were my own. The kids, all three girls, loved me and this made the parents happy. After working for about a week, my employer called the immigration lawyer in Manhattan and set up an appointment for me so we could begin the paperwork and I could have my work permit so I would not be working illegally. I met with the lawyer, I got my work permit and filed an application for my green card. It would take three to four years the lawyer informed me. I did not mind, I was in a good place and I was not breaking any laws. I knew in my heart that this was my path for bigger things for me in the future and I would make the sacrifices necessary to get there.

Living and working with this family was interesting, fun, and educational. They were very successful and rich, but did not inherit these riches. They both worked hard, made many sacrifices to get to this point, and they were still working hard and continued to make sacrifices to keep that success. I was an early riser, and Mr. B would be up earlier than me 5:00 am and go to his office on the third floor, and would work until 10:00 -11:00 pm at night. They were very hard workers. They were positive role models for their kids, their employees, and for me as well. They treated all their employees well; everyone loved working for this couple. Their success was earned. I learned by watching them. I enjoyed working here. I had a beautiful room overlooking the harbor in which I could see the boats passing by. The house had its own library. The library was stocked with all type of books, a lot of it historical reads. I took up reading and it became a hobby. When the girls were at school and I had completed my chores, I had so much free time that I would go to the library and read. I was reading two to three books per week. Then one day I asked Mr. B if I could use the computer in his office to type a letter to my parents. He said it was ok. One night after the kids were in bed I went to the office and began to type. I did not know that Mr. B was next door in his office. He heard me typing really fast and came by and stood at the door.

"I did not know that you could type, I was listening to the keys, and you type really fast," He said. I informed him that I was a typist and once did secretarial work in my country. He was amazed. The next day while everyone was having dinner, he spoke to Mrs. B.

"Did you know Rosalind could type? Why don't we give her part time work in the office so she will not lose her skills?" He said. They did and I now had two jobs. While the kids were at school and I was free, if they needed me in the office I would help out, and they did pay me.

The best part of working there was that I felt like I fit in. They were very down to earth people, I did not see or feel any prejudice, any racism, and did not see any type of bigotry. They had all type of people in their home. They treated everyone the same, they respected their staff, and their staff respected them. When I accompanied the kids to the town shopping area and they met their friends, they would introduce me as their friend and not their babysitter or nanny. One day their parents' accountants, who were also their friends, and their daughter came over to play with the younger of the girls. They were the same age. They were playing in the family room. I went there also and sat on the couch. The younger of the girls saw me and came over and jumped on me. I began to tickle her and she was hysterically laughing, then she kissed me on the cheek. Her friend saw that. They then proceeded to the kitchen to get a snack.

"How can you kiss a black person?" I heard her friend asking her.

"Rosalind is my friend," She responded. Then I thought to myself, *kids learn from what they see and taught, and most of the teachings and examples begin at their home. This was not displayed in this home. She did not see color. She saw me as a person she had fun with. So this must have come from the friend's home and what she saw.* I left it like that, did not inform the parents. Racism was something I was not used to even though I read the history of the U.S. and knew it was a big issue and that it still existed. As for me, I treated all equally and tried my best to get along with everyone as I believe we are one people and should live as such.

I had some fond memories working there. One of which I would never forget. The couple I worked for was away on business for a few days, and the butler went to Brooklyn on his day off. I was left with the three kids. The weather was bad that evening. The kids were all in the family room on the first floor watching TV and playing games. I went up to my room to get something and when I got to the 3rd floor, all the lights went off. Thunder and lightning, no electricity. The house was now pitch black, the alarm was going off. I had no candles, no flashlight. I heard screams and cries, so I ran downstairs to get the girls. The girls were all crying, all holding on tightly to my clothes making it difficult for me to walk. I tried to calm them and assured them that it was temporary and we would be alright. We all went upstairs and I took them to my room and they all cuddled up in bed together. I stayed with them for a few minutes until they calmed down and fell asleep. I did not know how long the lights would be out, did not know the code to turn the alarm off, and the only light I could see was from the phone. I knew their uncle's number so I dialed it and I asked for his help. He told me the code, so I was able to take the alarm off before the police came. He came over with a flashlight and candles, and stayed with us until the lights came back which was about two hours later. The girls phoned their parents the next day and told them what happened and how I handled it. The parents were pleased and relieved that everyone was ok and thanked me for keeping them safe.

I continued to work and live in Roslyn Harbor with this family until one day in late October I was informed by my lawyer that the immigration department had called my number and I had to return to Trinidad for my interview scheduled for November 15th, 1991, with the U.S. Consulate, to get my green card. I was eight months pregnant at this time, and my pregnancy from the beginning was a difficult one. I was having one problem after another, and had just returned to work after being on bed rest for bleeding episodes. At this time my placenta was not in place, and my doctor informed me that she would have to schedule a C-section when I was due. I informed her that I had to travel out of the country but she advised against it.

"It's too dangerous," She said. I waited four years, worked so hard for this day, and there was no way I was going to reschedule my interview with the immigration authorities. My gut was telling me to go for it. So I went with my gut, and traveled against medical advice. With all that was happening with my pregnancy, my stress level was high. This trip I thought would alleviate some of that stress, and it did. I did not see my family since leaving Trinidad four years ago. It was my first time back. At this time I was married and we both flew to Trinidad for our interview. No one in my family knew I was coming, I decided to surprise them. I knew everyone would be home on a Sunday as the family always got together on a Sunday. I arrived at my parent's home, walked up the stairs, entered the living room to first surprise my parents. Then all my sisters came rushing in when they heard my voice. The screams were so loud, half of the villagers came running to the house because they thought someone died or got hurt. My sisters all gathered around me and we began to jump for joy, then they played some Calypso music and we began to dance. My mother was screaming for me to stop as she feared the baby would come at that moment, but I was having a good time.

Despite having a rough pregnancy, I was driven on the roughest of roads to get to the beaches. I cannot swim, but went into the water just to take a dip and to taste the salt water. I had so much fun, I was happy. I spent one week in Trinidad. During that time I had my interview, all my paperwork was in order, and I was given my green card. I returned to NY and to the family that sponsored me. That would be my last week with them, as I could no longer care for their kids with a kid of my own on the way. They were expecting that and were very understanding and supportive. I said my goodbyes and left the great once strangers that now became my friends. I would never forget their kindness and generosity.

My due date per the doctor was the first week of January, 1992. I was now three weeks away from that day. It was the middle of December and I was almost nine months pregnant. It had snowed two days before. I was still driving because my stomach was not that big, even though I was so far in pregnancy. I was driving along Linden Boulevard on the service road around 6:00 pm, and it was dark. The roads were not wet and I did not see any snow on the road. I was heading west to Brooklyn from Queens, when I lost control of my car, the car left the road, jumped the pavement into the main road, (a three lane type highway), spun a couple times, turned eastward, then re-jumped the pavement back onto the service road before coming to a stop. When it went into the main road, thank God the vehicles were stopped for the red light about five hundred feet away, causing them to approach slowly, just before it re-jumped the pavement back to the service road as a truck was approaching. When I saw this I began to scream, *Oh my god, oh my god!* If the car did not re-jump and remove itself from that main road facing in the direction of the oncoming vehicles, I could not imagine the disaster that would have been. When the car came to a complete stop, I was shaking uncontrollably, and crying hysterically. Someone came over to my aid and called for help. They took me to the hospital. I was examined, they took an ultrasound, and found the baby to be fine, and when my obstetrician came in, she looked at me, unsure of what was happening.

"You sure live dangerously, but this time it paid off, your placenta is back in place and you can have a natural delivery," She said. I later learned from the police report that it was black ice I must have drove on.

I did not drive after that until after delivery. When I was not driving I was running for the bus. It was now the holidays, and I was still going to parties and dancing. With all this hyperactivity my baby was doing fine. The night of December 30th, I had some friends over at my apartment. We were eating, talking, dancing, and having a good time. Before everyone left I began to have intermittent pain, and then it came frequently. I did not know what contractions felt like as it was my first pregnancy so I called my friend Kamala and told her my symptoms. She told me to take a shower and prepare to go to the hospital, the baby was most likely coming. It was now 11 am December 31st, New Years Eve. My husband had to go to different party venues to set up their music, he was a self employed electronic technician, and this was the busiest day of the year for him. I lived in Brooklyn, my doctor and hospital for delivery was in Long Island, a thirty minute ride away. My husband did not drive therefore I had to call one of our friends Clarke to take me to the hospital. When I got to the hospital and they examined me, I had only opened up four centimeters. They said they were discharging me, I must return home. I somehow knew that today was the day I would deliver. I fought with them, asked them to keep me, told them I would do whatever it took. I lived too far and by the time I get home I would have to turn around and come right back. They listened to me and admitted me and told me to walk around the hospital. Clarke left me there. I was there all alone. I began to walk around the hospital like they told me.

I walked for about forty five minutes, then sat for a minute. As I sat, a young couple came over and asked me if I was ok. I told them I was in labor but I would be ok. They then asked if they could pray with me. I said yes. They prayed with me for a few minutes. I then got up and continued to walk. After walking for about two hours I returned to labor and delivery. I had now opened up seven centimeters and they began to prepare for delivery. I laid there for a while with not much movement from the baby. It was New Year's Eve and the doctors perhaps wanted to get out in time to celebrate the New Year with their love ones, and I understood that. They then decided to induce me, and after induction, the pain was increasing and they gave me an epidural before delivery and a little while later at 9:30pm on December 31st, my son was born. He was healthy with ten fingers and ten toes, and that's all that mattered at that time. When they held him in front of me, the first thing I thought was *Did I make that?* He was born with so much hair, jet black, and straight. After delivery I was so hungry, I had not eaten anything for twenty four hours. I begged any and every one that came by for something to eat, but all said the kitchen was closed, everyone was gone, and that they did not have anything. This one older nurse came and said to me don't worry I will find you something. I did not know what it took, but what I do know is that she went out of her way for me. When she came back she came back with soup, crackers and juices. I was so thankful. I could not stop thanking her, and did not forget this kind gesture.

Chapter 15

Unconventional Marriage

I got married in 1988 in Brooklyn NY, by the Justice of Peace. It was an unconventional marriage. In my opinion this guy was not husband material and I was not in love with him. Then why did I marry him? He was a friend and he needed my help, and since I was in a position to help this friend and his teenage child who lived in Trinidad, I did. This child of his was travelling down a very dark and dangerous path, and I believed I was used by God to serve a particular purpose in their lives and when that purpose was served I would make my exit and move forward with my life. It was agreed by both of us that this marriage came with an expiration date. I knew it would take at most ten years to serve the purpose. However not only did I serve the purpose, I was taught a valid lesson.

My mission was to save this child, take him away from that dangerous path and stare him in a different and safer direction. I made the necessary sacrifice to get this child into the United States, the land of opportunity. The land where anyone can make it if they desire to, which would give him the opportunity of a better life and to make something great out of it for himself. He was given the resources needed to succeed. Instead of taking advantage of the opportunities given, he did the opposite. After getting here and becoming acquainted with his environment he attempted to do the right thing, but eventually chose to continue on the path of self destruction that he was so well familiarized with.

While serving this purpose I was blessed with a child of my own. This was not in my plan, perhaps in God's, but was very much welcomed and a blessing. Despite knowing the marriage came with an expiration date, we had an amicable relationship. I bought a home in Queens Village where we all resided. His son got his green card he came to live with us. The process took eight years and he lived with us for two. During the period of time he lived with us, I was observing my ex's parenting skills. It was quite obvious that this was a bit challenging for him, as he tried to guide and discipline this child. However I am a strong disciplinarian, taught well by my father; therefore I laid the rules, provided guidance and appropriate discipline when needed. He was not used to that, therefore I became a monster in his eyes, while the father did not do much to stop this child's self destructive path, and soon it became a very toxic environment for myself and our son Kyle. I did all that I could do to help this child, but when it became evident to me that he did not want to be help or saved, it was time for me to make my exit. The lesson learned was that you cannot help someone who does not want to be helped. But guilt and sadness soon consumed me as I learned that two years later he was killed. He had kept bad company and the things that he did got him killed. I did have question as to why God used me in this way but not sure if I ever found the answers.

When I informed my then husband that I was ready for the divorce, he became very angry because he now realized that he was losing everything that was good in his life. While we were married I was good to him and his son. Now it was time for me to advance myself and build a greater life for myself and my son. I had to put my house on the market and when reality hit him he became furious and threatened to burn the house down. I did not allow that threat to deter me. I have been built with strong faith and I feared no man but God. I have great confidence in myself and my abilities and regardless of what he did I knew I would rebuild as long as there was no physical harm to my son nor myself. I was not worried about the material things. I went ahead and placed my house on the market; it went fast because I had recently done major improvements. I made a profit on the sale. I then rented an apartment in a private house not too far from where we lived so that Kyle would remain in the same school and so my single motherhood life began.

THE COURAGEOUS MOTHER
By
ROSALIND NOREIGA

A mother learned that her only son was killed

He died in an accident, they say doing what

he loved, riding his motorcycle

He was young, just beginning life, at age 25, gone so soon

The day had come, she had to lay her child to rest

But this child was not any child. This child was a soldier

A soldier in the U.S. military and a soldier in God's army

She must now say goodbye

A mother should not have to bury her child everyone says

The casket laid in the center of the church

The church is full, standing room only both

inside and outside of the church

One speaker after another told of what a great person he was

His sister played the piano with her back to the keys, facing the

audience, just the way he liked to watch her play. The entire

congregation is now in tears. There is not a dry eye in the church

Then his mother gathered her two remaining children,

the two daughters, and her husband and stood

next to the casket. She was about to speak

The mom herself, a soldier in the U.S. military, and a

soldier in God's army. They are a Christian family

She said to the congregation "Don't cry, dry those tears,

and let's celebrate my son's life, he is in our father in

heaven's hands now. He is safe, he is at peace"

She is so calm, no tears in her eyes. She is smiling,

she stands tall and so strong, how can that be?

You see, she is a devoted Christian and that courage she displayed in front of her son's coffin, in front of all those people, she drew it from her great faith. Through that faith, one can see a profound trust in the God she serves and believes in. And she asked us to do the same. What a courageous mother I say

Chapter 16

Single Motherhood

Kyle was around seven years old at the time of the separation and eight when we got the divorce. The first thing I did as a single mom was take my son on a much needed vacation, so I took him to Disney World. It was time for us both to have some fun together. We stayed at Disney World for an entire week, went through all the parks and we had the time of our lives. I realized that the challenges ahead, raising a child all by myself in a big city like NY might be great, now that I have to be both mother and father to him. I knew I may not be able to teach a boy to be a man, this was a part better served by a male figure, but I was going to do the best that I could to surround him with positive male role models like his now deceased godfather Anthony. May his soul rest in peace.

I now needed to hire a babysitter to take Kyle to and from school while I was at work. I found one who lived about two blocks away from the school and worked opposite the school as a hairdresser. She also had a son the same age as my son and attended the same school. It was easy for me to drop him off at her house on my way to work, and she walked them to school and back to her house after school where I would pick him up after work. This arrangement worked well for a while, until one day my son informed me that he and her son were walking to school by themselves. This was concerning to me especially since they had to cross a major intersection on their way to get to school. There was sometimes a crossing guard but this was not safe to me. I evaluated my situation and decided what would be best for us would be to be closer to family and friends where we could get the support we needed. Two of my sisters were living in Maryland at this time and his godparents. I spoke to his godmother Sherma first, and she suggested we live in her mother's basement apartment until we found a bigger apartment. She spoke to her mom about it and her mom agreed to rent it to us. Her mom lived upstairs and this was good I thought because she could keep an eye on him for the hour when I left for work and before he leaves for school and the hour after he gets back before I return home from work. She was retired. And so the decision to relocate to Maryland was made. I knew as a single parent the changing of many addresses may be necessary and I was prepared for it. We moved from New York in the summer of 2000 and Lanham, Maryland became our new address. Moving was not new to me to. At this point I had already lived at six different addresses. But it was a bit new for my son. However, he adjusted well after leaving our home to the first apartment.

The best thing about our new location was that the elementary school was located behind the house about one block away, and there was a walk path with houses on either side of the path. The neighborhood children used this path to get to school. No vehicle traffic. It was a safe walk to school, and Kyle was able to do this by himself as the neighbors knew each other and sat on their porches in the morning and evening when the kids are walking to and from school, keeping an eye on them. This made me feel better. Kyle was only eight at this time but acted more mature for his age. He listened to me, obeyed, and continued to do well at school. Ever since kindergarten he was tested and placed in the Talented and Gifted (TAG) program. A program he maintained his space in all the way through junior high school.

As he was an only child, I had to find activities after school and during the weekend to keep him engaged and socializing. I enrolled him in basketball classes, tennis classes, swimming, and karate. I got him a library card and reading became one of his hobbies that I most certainly welcomed. What was amazing and gratifying for me was that he used all the resources given to him and that kept him on top of his class. He was student of the month every single month of his elementary school year, and at the end of his elementary school year he was awarded the principal award and student of the year.

As a single mother raising a boy, I knew I had to lay a very solid foundation for him, one built with discipline, values, and rules that would help him through to adulthood. And I did. I was tough when I needed to be tough, supportive and encouraging, and engaging. I provided guidance and made him the priority of my life. We did a lot together, I played basketball with him, tennis with him, took him to the track with me and we would compete in a hundred meter dash. When he had karate tournaments to advance from one belt to another, I would help him at home practice his moves to have him well prepared for the tournament. On the day of one of his tournaments, after he demonstrated his skills to the judges, his karate instructor had a word with him.

"Did your dad work with you on those moves? You have become better at it," The instructor said.

"No it was my mom that worked with me on it," Kyle answered. The instructor then looked at me perplexed and smiled.

"Good job mom," He said. I remember one day I took him to the movies. He wanted to see a karate film, a comedy type called "Kung Pow." To him it was funny and the best film, he was laughing and enjoying it, while I was bored out of my mind, it was such an agonizing ninety minutes for me. "Kyle what a stupid movie," I would say.

"Mom it's funny, you just don't get it," he replied. He enjoyed it and I guess that's all that mattered. When he was not with me, he was with his aunts and godparents. He now had the support he needed.

After my son graduated from elementary school he was sent to a middle school in the TAG program. Once a child is in the TAG program they will be given bus transportation to that school regardless of where they live. Kyle was growing and we needed more living space, and here we go again, I had to move. After two years in Lanham, we were moving to Greenbelt, a five minute ride away. I rented a bigger one bedroom apartment with more living space in a garden apartment building. The school bus would pick him up and drop him off in front of the apartment to and from school. I was now in the nursing program and still working full time so my days were very hectic. Then, at ten and a half years old, I was able to leave him by himself for a couple of hours while I was at school. He was really a well behaved and a discipline child. He had proven that he could be trusted. I continued to work and now in the nursing program the work load had increased. The last six months of the program I had to quit my job, and put all my focus in successfully completing the program. Juggling school, work, and parenting at times was a struggle. Financially, I was drained and struggling to keep food on the table for us. Physically and emotionally, it began to take a toll on me. I was only averaging two to three hours of sleep per night. Just when I began to worry I got a very nice surprise. One day, when I picked up my mails, in between the bills I found a card from Candida. As I opened the envelope, the card read, thinking of you my friend. When I opened it there was a check for five hundred dollars, and a note which read:

"I know that you are not working and in school, and that things might be a little tough right now, I also know that you would not ask for help, but here is a little something to help you and Kyle until you are back on your feet, and that will be soon," She stated. What a blessing. These are some of the resources God has placed in my life. at times I did not always use it. This kind gesture reminded me that I should not let pride stand in my way which is what I perhaps was doing.

In 2005, we both graduated, I from my nursing program, and Kyle from junior high. It was during his graduation that we both were quite amazed when they announced his name as the Presidential Award winner for excellence throughout his schooling from kindergarten to the end of junior high. They kept track of his performances. We were both shocked, he could barely move, and my entire body was chilled, goosebumps. Then his teacher came over and walked him up to the podium to receive his award that was hand delivered by the Senator from Maryland. The tears were just flowing from my eyes. I could hear myself saying, *Our hard work has paid off, I must give myself a pat on the back, I am doing a good job, thank you God.* I kept the faith; I did not let anything or anyone come between us. I was on a mission to achieve our goals. I had no social life, I made many sacrifices. This was by far the best moment in my life. His teacher later apologized for not informing us, but explained that they wanted it to be a surprise and told me how much she enjoyed having him in her class. This was such a proud moment for a mother. Just then the memory of his brother surfaced, and silently I said to myself, *We might have failed and lost one but that period of darkness is fading and is making way for the light to shine brightly in our lives now.*

Now Kyle got the presidential award when he graduated, what I got was a transmission that decided that this is the day it would die on me. On my graduation day, I did not have a car, but I did not let that damper my spirits. My girl Candida and her husband John came down from NY to my graduation. They drove me and we all had a great celebratory time. When I was worried about how I would get around now that I had to find a job, Jackie came by.

"You are a nurse now, and there is a nursing shortage. You will be hired in no time, let's go get a car," She said.

"Jackie I have no money, how would I get a car?" I said.

"Let's go, you don't have to put any money down," She said. So we went to Toyota, they checked my credit, and the sales person came back to me smiling.

"My boss said I can sell you anything you want, you can buy the entire lot of cars if you want because your credit is so damn good and you don't need any money down," He said. I was so amazed and thankful for the continuous blessing I had been receiving.

Now that he was a teenager and began high school, it was time to give Kyle his privacy, his own room. I now needed a two bedroom apartment, and so it was time to pack up and move yet again. Here was my life in constant motion. I was now working as an RN and receiving a better income, therefore I was able to move into a beautiful two bed/ two bath huge apartment located opposite the high school he would attend, Eleanor Roosevelt High School, in Greenbelt. At the end of the first semester in high school, he earned a 4.0 GPA that gained him student of the month award. I continued to provide the support and guidance that he needed. But now I began to see the changes as he was now a teenager. Before high school we did so much together, but now he did not want to be seen with his mom. If I dropped him off to meet his friends, I could no longer kiss him. One day I told him to come to the school track with me so we could run and do some exercises. He agreed to come but he wanted me to get a head start, because he did not want to be seen walking with his mom to the track. I understood his dilemma somewhat, however I still purposely did it to see his reaction.

One day I was driving him and his friends to the movies and one of my favorite songs was playing on the radio, so I turned up the volume and began dancing and singing loud while driving and attempted to engage him and his friends, when I looked at him he seemed embarrassed.

"Mom you are embarrassing me," He said. I laughed. A few weeks later he came back to me about the same topic.

"Mom my friends like you they thinks that you are cool," He said.

"You see, and you were embarrassed of your mother, I am the cool mom-go mommy, it's your birthday," I teased.

Kyle was in high school now, and did not need me as much so it was time for me to have a social life, get on the dating seen. I had not truly dated much in my life because I did not care too much for kissing many frogs before meeting my prince charming. I believed in a strong relationship with one person, so I was looking to get directly to my prince charming. This was 2006, and who knew what was out there, therefore I was a bit skeptical, cautious, and did not want to just put myself out there. I told my best friend Candida about my dilemma and she suggested E-harmony, online dating.

"This site is strictly relationship based and I know a few people who used this site and had successful relationships," She informed me. And so I went online to E-Harmony and found some good matches, but one stood out more than the others, he stood out because I was not looking for a couch potato as I am an athlete, and based on his profile he was an athlete also. He was a body builder, personal trainer, and into physical fitness and he had what I was looking for. We did not put photos of ourselves on our profile on E-harmony, therefore we did not know what each other looked like. I connected and communicated with him via emails through E-harmony until I felt comfortable enough to give him my phone number. He called. We spoke for a few weeks and got to know each other by many long phone conversations before meeting in person. We set a date, and met at a Barnes and Noble bookstore at a town center mall in Maryland.

I got there first and waited for him as he was coming from Virginia to Maryland to meet me. He came dressed in athletic clothing which showed off his well built physique. Honestly that did not impress me. Yes he looked great but what got my attention and impressed me was his confidence that came through while walking towards me and his mannerisms. When I placed my hand out to shake his when introducing myself, he instead open his arms and warmly embrace me with a hug.

"My mama taught me not to shake a lady's hand but to hug a lady instead," He stated. He was also a gentleman, opened doors, and pulled the chair out and seated me before he sat. We talked for a while about everything from current events, to physical fitness, to politics, and people. With that confidence he carried I could feel the positive energy that flowed. When I dropped a negative he would immediately give it a positive spin and always saw things in a different perspective. What really impressed me was what he did and continues to do up to this day, that is when we sat to have lunch he leaned over and asked if he can take my hand and if we can pray together to bless the food. I had never done this before, and appreciated this and we held hands and prayed before eating. After having lunch we walked around the mall, talking and getting to know each other. Although it was our first date, it felt like we knew each other all our lives, we were talking and laughing and feeling comfortable with each other. This first date lasted four hours, but it did not disappoint.

The chemistry was most definitely there. We went on many dates after that and a special relationship developed between us. And twelve years later we are still talking and laughing a lot and enjoying each other's company, and he is still opening car doors for me. What we later discovered is that I am the female version of him and he is the male version of me. We are so much alike, and have so much in common; even our birthdays are three days from each other in the same month. Since I found Robert to be the person that I could relate to, the one that keeps me laughing, the one I fell in love with and has built a good relationship with, he became my prince charming and as a result I did not have to kiss any frogs.

Kyle was about to graduate from high school and four months before his graduation date, it was time to move yet again. This time the move was to our own home. I purchased a single family home in Lanham, and yes we moved back to Lanham, Maryland. I was amazed to see that Kyle did not fuss each time I told him we were moving, he just would say okay mom, and start packing, and with each move he easily adjusted, and life became better for both of us. He graduated from high school as a History scholar, from a program that he entered at the beginning of his high school year and stayed in throughout. I had a graduation party and house warming party together for us, and so we celebrated with friends and family our achievements.

He was accepted in a few colleges but chose one closer to home. However he lived in the dorm. And just when I thought my nest was empty and that in four years after graduation he would be fully on his own and would have the house all to myself and was about to have a celebration of my own, he came right back home after only one year of college. I was disappointed with his performance and his disrespect towards me when I expressed my dissatisfaction. Oh boy how I wanted to hurt him! I was livid. How could he not see that all the sacrifices I made as a single mother was for him. Why? Why? Why? I had so many questions with few answers.

"When they are small you will have small problems, when they are big, the problems you may have to deal with becomes much bigger," Were words spoken by my mother. She was not lying, I thought, because the problems were huge. Motherhood in itself is a difficult job, but single motherhood is twice as difficult for both the mother and the child. I did not know which way to turn, how to help him anymore. I wanted to turn my back and let him face the consequences on his own and teach him a lesson. But I could not. I could not fail this one too. I was in a position to help. We had a serious talk. He apologized to me and promised he would redeem himself. However he still needed my help. After wasting twenty five thousand on tuition, I was not sure if I wanted to take that gamble. I thought long and hard about it and concluded that everyone deserved a second chance, therefore I gave him one. He did redeemed himself by going back to school and working to help pay for his tuition and finally he got a degree, not the one he first set out to get, but he got one. And now at 26 he is finally on his own and doing ok for himself.

Chapter 17

Running

Running is a hobby I acquired while growing up in Trinidad. Having to work the farmland located three miles away from our home with my parents, we often walked behind my father while he rode his bicycle. Walking for me was too slow and boring so I would opt for running behind him instead. My father owned twenty five acres of farmland, some of which was on hills. Some of the best fruits and produce were on the hilly part of the land. I would run up the hill in spite of my mother telling me not too. I enjoyed it and became so well at it that I used it to escape from my father when I disobeyed him, which was very often. I was a bit rude, defiant, and downright stubborn. When my father told me to do something or say something that I disagreed with, I would answer him back which was forbidden in my home as my father was the law and you do not disobey the law. Often times when I was rude to him I knew a slap would be coming or whatever he got his hands on he would let me have it; therefore I would run after I said something smart to him, knowing that he would chase me down until he found me and whipped my butt. At times, he would chase me through the neighborhood. This practice was well watched and became an amusement to the neighbors. This was a challenge I welcomed because it just meant that his chase would allow me to increase in speed.

As running became a passion during my junior high school years, I signed up for physical education. I did every sport available to me, from gymnastics to net ball, to track and field and amazingly I did great in all. But track and field is where I shined the most especially in sprint. I became a sprinter mastering the one hundred to one hundred and fifty meter dashes. I represented my class during competitions among the different grades of classes, as I was one of the fastest runners in the school. My classmates gave me the nickname "Racehorse." When I asked Shane, the brightest boy in the class, why "Racehorse" he said:

"I say racehorse because if you watch a horse run, it never looks back, and as soon as the buzzer goes off, it reaches the finish line at a blink of an eye. That's you." He was right. I never looked back when running or walking and the reason for that is because my mother told a story from the Bible about Lot's wife that when she looked back, she turned into a pillar of salt. That forever stuck with me, and as a child I believed it would happen if I looked back. Silly, but it felt so real to me.

In track and field, my next best performance on the track was the high jump. I remember during a competition in my third year of junior high I got the gold medal in high jump. I jumped five feet two inches without once touching the bar. Now I loved running and all my medals I gave to my mother to keep for me, but the medal I won for the high jump I kept it around my neck for a while because I was so proud of this achievement. It was a very clean jump. One day my mother sent me to the corner shop from my home to get some food. I forgot I was wearing the medal, but the owner Mr. Johnson saw it and asked about it. A few weeks later he happened to be fencing his yard. The fence was taller than six feet in height. My father asked him why he was placing the fence so high.

"Your daughter is jumping over five feet, so I figure I have to go much higher than five feet," He said to my father. My father laughed so hard when he told me this. After that day I gave my mother the medal I received for jumping to keep also.

I was doing so well in running that my coach selected me to try out for regionals and then nationals. My father acquired asthma while serving in the military, and lived with asthma for the rest of his life. One day, after running practice, when I got home I began to wheeze and was a bit short of breath. My father saw this. When I asked his permission to compete in regionals he said no I cannot run anymore because I have asthma. He did not take me to the doctor, it was a onetime incident, but he diagnosed me with asthma and that was his final decision. Like I said my father was the law and as much I wanted to go against this one, I could not. My running at school came to a halt. But it continued periodically at home. In the 1970's, during my teenage years, during the Easter holidays and summer vacations, the churches and several different organizations in the village would host large sporting events in which the nearby villages would participate and prizes would be offered to the winners. Those games my entire family would attend and participate. I would win every race I entered. I remember one of my former elementary school classmates would be at the race. Her legs were longer than mines but I was faster than her. If she saw me line up to run a race she would not enter the race because she wanted to win first prize and knowing I was in it, she does not stand a chance. My mother would also win the races she entered, so by the end of the event almost all the first place prizes went to the Brewsters, my family.

In high school I ran a little but did not compete much. After high school the running stopped for a while. I often wondered if I was not stopped how far I could have gone. It resumed when I migrated to the United States and lived in NY, but changed from sprinting gradually to long distance. When I lived in Queens Village NY, I would go to the nearby school tracks and run around the tracks. I did not know how to pace myself in running. I always ran sprint, therefore I had to learn to pace myself. Then one day I saw an advertisement of an upcoming five mile race in Hempstead Long Island, not too far from Queens Village. I decided to attend that race. In most of these races the goal is to raise funds for charity and I love participating in charitable events. I wasn't sure if I was prepared but entered the race anyway. The morning of the five mile run, I lined up like everyone else. In the line I met a Caucasian male in his fifties and we began to talk. I found out that he was a scientist. He asked me if I ever did a long distance run before and I told him no. He then advised me to take off very slowly and build speed, and to pace myself. This was new for me and I truly didn't know how to do that, but was willing to try. The buzzer went off and I took off like lightening forgetting or ignoring the advice I just received, and got burnt quickly. But before burning out, I ran past a young Caucasian couple. When I passed by them I heard the woman say:

"They are monkeys, they are used to swinging on trees so they are fast," Referring to me. This was a cultural shock for me. Being from a county where I grew up with all different races, cultures, and a variety of religion, racism was not something I was used to. I was tempted to stop and say something but I left it alone and continued running, *You can't change ignorance.* At the third mile, I felt burnt out and was struggling, so I decided to walk a little. While walking, an old Caucasian man passed me, he looked like he was in his eighties. While passing me he said:

"Don't quit now, make it to the finish line, you can do it!" And he continued running. Seeing this older man doing it, pacing himself, I first felt stupid. But seeing him not stopping and giving it all he had, it inspired me to continue and finish the race. I did make it to the finish line. At the finish line I met the older man who introduced himself as Willie. Willie, I learned, was eighty five years old and had been running for more than sixty years. Willie became my inspiration and from that day on I was pacing myself and decided to prepare for the next one as this was a yearly event. The next year I signed up for the same race and did not see Willie, when I asked about him, people who knew him very well informed me that he had passed away one week after the last race. I decided right there and then that I was going to do this race for Willie. I found myself running at a pace of eight minutes per mile and maintaining that speed all the way to the end. At the spot where Willie had passed me in the first race, I stopped for a moment of silence in honor of Willie. In life we never know who will be our influence and sometimes it may just be a humble stranger like Willie.

For many years while living in NY I continued to run small long distance races like 5ks, 10ks, and ten mile races. My ultimate goal was to run a marathon but had no idea how to prepare for a marathon of 26.2 miles. Thirteen years later, and I moved to Maryland with my son Kyle. After settling down and completing my nursing degree I began to pursue running a marathon. One day, I was on the Orange line from Maryland to D.C., when an advertisement on the train caught my attention. It was from the AIDs Foundation, an organization that raised funds for the Whitman Walker Clinic in D.C. and a clinic that provided free healthcare services to those who had no insurance and were struck by HIV/AIDS. They were seeking people to raise funds and they would train you to run the next marathon they would be participating in which was the ING Marathon in Miami on Jan 28th, 2007. Their contact information was printed on the advertisement.

When I got home, I immediately went online and got the necessary information. I learned from the info that I needed to raise twenty five hundred dollars. I saw the ad in September of 2006, and the deadline to turn in the funds was November 1st, 2006. This only gave me two months. Got to move fast I thought. It also stated that hotel rooms would be paid for by them and fifty percent of the air fare would be given. They would train you every Saturday for three months through their AIDs Training Program. I registered online and began training at the end of September with other runners. They placed us in running groups according to our pace time. I was pacing eight minutes per mile at the time, therefore I was placed in the eight to ten per mile pace group. The first day we ran six miles and each week it would increase by two miles.

I wanted to do this, therefore I had to raise the money. I do not like asking people for money because I feel like its begging, but I wanted this so I had to swallow my pride, and just beg if I had to. I decided I would use all my resources to help me pull this off. One of my sisters was self employed with several clients, and my other sister worked for Metro. I gave both of them donation forms and asked them to collect donations for me. They did and it got me most of the money raised. At the time, I was at my first nursing job at a hospital nearby. I took my form to work and asked each and every one I came across for donations.

"I am running for this charity I need sponsors, it's 26.2 miles and I need a different sponsors for each mile, whatever you can give would be appreciated," I would say. Within three weeks, I raised thirty two hundred dollars. Seven hundred more than what was required for my trip to Miami and entering the race. If the required amount was not raised, you could not continue to train through the AIDs training program. One of the girls in my running group always dreamed of running a marathon. She did not reach the amount needed and the deadline was soon approaching. I asked the program director if I could give her my excess seven hundred so she could attend. He said yes, so I did and she was so excited and appreciative. Now that I had secured my place in the group to run for the AIDs foundation, I was more focused now on running the twenty three miles. Before leaving for Miami to complete our training, we first had to do our own marathon given to us by the Aids Training Program. We had to run twenty three miles with completion if we were to survive the 26.2. We all did and completed the twenty three miles, two weeks before the big marathon. It was my first and I was so looking forward to it.

On January 28th, 2007 I woke up at 3:00 am in a hotel room near South Beach in Miami. Lineup was at 5:00 am and the race began at 6:00 am. My roommate was a younger woman and since everyone had a story behind why they were running, I asked her hers. She told me hers was her desire to lose weight to look slimmer for her wedding day which was fast approaching. She was doing the half marathon, 13.1 miles. The morning of, she was doubtful as to whether she could do it, especially since her time was not so great. I gave her a pep talk. I said to her endurance is the name of the game, do not worry so much about what time you finish, focus on enduring the journey so you can make it to the finish line. We all left the hotel together as a group and got to the line-up at 4:45 am. At 5:30 am the rain began to fall; at times being very hard downpour of showers. We were in line with tens of thousands of people and were all trapped with no way out, no choice but to get wet. We were soaked to the bone but that did not stop anyone from running. The buzzer went off at exactly 6:00 am and the ING Marathon of 2007 began. We would be running along Dade County. Within ten minutes of starting the race, the sun was out in all its glory and the humidity began to kick our ass. I started good, we tried to stay in our familiar pace groups keeping our pace steady until around the half way point, the 13.1 mile marker, where everyone began to run their own race.

To my amusement I saw a little bit of everything in this being my first marathon, from the way participants were dressed weird, to finding a bathroom which was very challenging. Many went to the bushes to do their thing; some did it on themselves and had to be hosed down by spectators. One thing I saw at around the tenth mile that was very concerning was a big tall guy began to move around in circles, and then began to drift from side to side. When I looked at him closely, he looked somewhat dazed, and I immediately yelled to my fellow runners that he was going to fall, needed help, and for someone to call the paramedics. Soon after my screams, many runners stopped and we all caught him before he hit the concrete. He was definitely having a medical emergency. When the paramedics came, those of us who stopped to help him then continued our race. If you are not an elite runner competing for the top three prizes or spots, you are more competing against yourself to beat your previous marathon finish time. Therefore it was truly nice to see the human spirit in all its glory along the course, especially when the fellow runner was experiencing a problem; that they stopped and helped them along the way. Though most of us are strangers to each other we did run as a team for one cause, charity. It did not matter which charity at the end of the race since most of the proceeds go to charities. What was more fascinating and incredible to me was seeing people of all types of handicap not letting their handicap stop them. There were one legged runners, no arm runners, runners running on mechanical legs, wheelchair runners; and they all made it to the finish line. It's amazing what one can do when they put their minds to it. On marathon day, endurance is the name of the game and many prove that they do have what it takes. It was so great to see.

Along the race route there were many spectators cheering us on, mostly strangers. They were out offering water, chips, fruits like oranges, even beers and liquor which I was surprised to see some runners stop and take. I appreciated the oranges because they were so sweet and I got to replace some of my electrolytes. At the 13.1 mile, the half way point, I was doing well with a time of two hours and thirteen minutes. *I am in good shape,* I told myself. But what really got me going at the fifteen mile mark was a musical band with drums and a host of other musical instruments. As I approached they were playing Latin music. Wow! Wow! Music to my ears I was saying. I stopped in front of the band in the middle of my race and began to dance the salsa. One of the men nearby joined me and we became a couple dancing the salsa in the middle of a race. Oh this is so much fun. If all marathons are like this, I can run a marathon every week I told myself.

I continued to run and at the 20th mile the buildup of lactic acid in my legs got the better of me. My legs began to cramp up, it felt so stiff and painful, and it stopped me in my tracks. I stretched; I had some salt packets on me and placed some salt under my tongue, drank some water and tried to walk it out for the next mile. It began to feel better so I continued to run with my goal of making it to the finish line heavy on my mind. At the 23rd mile it hit me again, this time everything was cramping and my butt was hurting so badly. It is then I remembered what Oprah Winfrey said on her show after she completed her first NYC marathon. I remember her saying "at the 23rd mile is when you start seeing Jesus." And she was absolutely right, I began to call upon him to see me through to the finish line. I was so close, I did not want to give up; I can't give up after making it this far. I did not give up, I slowed down and decreased my speed. I made it to the finish line with so much jubilance you would think that I just began the race. *Mission accomplished*, I thought.

The ING Marathon set the stage for many more to come. Nine months later, I registered for the Marine Corps Marathon in Washington DC. This time training on my own, using the tools obtained from the AIDS Training Program. I trained by running in the streets around the nearby cities to my home, running six to ten miles per day, then increasing by three miles weekly until I completed at least 23 miles before marathon day. I began running at 5:00 am and if it was not during the summer where 5:00 am was a bit dark, I would run not on the sidewalks but in the middle of the street where it was lighted and could be seen. At that time of the morning, not many cars were on the street. One day I was running along Greenbelt road heading to College Park in Maryland and was approaching under a bridge that had a lot of bushes on either side and a secluded area where homeless people occupied; I stayed in the middle of the street only to have a car come from behind, and this was not just any car, but the police, a distance away from me. They got on their bull horns and shouted, get off the road, get off the road, run on the side walk. I did as they told, waved to them, and when they were out of sight I went right back to running in the middle of the street where I felt safer until I reached an area where it was safe again to run on the sidewalks. I would take the same route each time I ran.

One day, while driving, I stopped for gas at a local gas station only to hear the gas attendant say "You are the girl that runs on Greenbelt road every day, I see you all the time, and you are a good runner!'" From that day I decided to change my route each time, because safety was my first priority. Training did not consist of only running, but a good diet, weight lifting, and meditating. To complete a marathon you have to be both physically and mentally prepared. It was October 22nd, 2007 my birthday weekend, and I was lined up in Roslyn, Virginia with about twenty thousand runners for the Marine Corps marathon. This being my second was quite as challenging, but I managed it better than the first, and enjoyed it just as much.

After completing my second marathon within ten months I set a goal to complete at least five marathons before the age of 50. I began the first at forty four that gave me six years. My next one was set for

March 2008, in the dead of winter in D.C. I was registered for the Sun Trust D.C. marathon. I continued to train and completed that one too. Now I had completed three marathons within fifteen months and it was time to give my body a break. *I will tone it down*, I kept saying to myself. The love for running did not keep me away. I was participating only in shorter distances, 5ks, 10ks, 10 milers and occasionally half marathons. I did this for about four years.

After running for so long by myself I wanted to find a running buddy to train and run other races with. I went online but was unsuccessful as I was not looking for a love interest but strictly a running partner. So I gave up trying to find one. One day after entering and completing the Maryland University half marathon, and socializing at an Irish pub where they kept the race after-party, I met Carlene. She was also a lone runner but did not do full marathons. We talked for a while and she asked if we could run together. My heart and head was smiling and was saying ask and you shall receive; patience is a good thing to have. We exchanged numbers, met, ran together, enjoyed each other companies, and a friendship was born. Now we are great friends and have been running together since. Not only did we learn that we have good running chemistry together, but that our birthdays are one day from each other; so now we run and celebrate our birthdays together by doing our next best thing-dancing.

My 50th birthday was approaching and I had not completed the goal I set for myself. In the spring of the year of my 50th, I entered the Maryland University Annual half marathon for the second time. Normally I would complete a half marathon with a time of two hours and twenty minutes. But on this day I was struggling, I was having a very difficult time maintaining my pace. I had to stop many times and walk until I got my breathing normal, as I was experiencing shortness of breath and just felt weak and tired. This had not happened to me before during a race. I felt bad for Carlene because I interrupted her timing, although I begged her to run her race and that it was ok to leave me alone, I would be fine. She did not, she stopped when I stopped and ran when I ran. What a friend I thought. I do not begin something that I could not finish. Quitting is not in my DNA, so I finished the race at a time of greater than three hours. It was horrible for me, but I was ok. After I got home I was fine after sleeping for a while.

It was now my 50th birthday and I celebrated on the beaches in beautiful Barbados. I spent a week in Barbados and was returning on the day hurricane Sandy was approaching the North East. I had the worst flight ever; the plane took so much turbulence that I thought it would be blown out of the sky. I truly thought I was going to die on this plane, but then I began to pray and was thankful that at least I lived to be fifty and was able to celebrate it. We landed safely after a very, very rough flight. A couple days later I was returning to work. I parked where I normally park at work and walked up the flight of stairs as I always do only to experience shortness of breath and chest pain when I got to the top. I went to my unit on the 7th floor and placed my stuff in my locker. Before beginning work, I took one of the PCT's with me to the clean utility room where all the medical equipment was. I undressed and asked her to take an EKG on me. She did and when I looked at it and read it, it was abnormal. I could not tell exactly what was happening so I took it to one of the third year cardiology residents and asked him to interpret it for me. He said it was not good, but it was not that bad and advised me to see a cardiologist as soon as possible. At this age I did not even have a primary care physician because I never had the need for one. I do not take medications. I get the flu every year but refuse to take the flu shot and I let it take its course. I will drink lots of fluids when I get it to prevent dehydration but I do not take any over the counter flu meds nor antibiotics. If I am in pain, I will rest and will not even take

a Tylenol. One of my colleagues recommended a specific cardiologist.
I made an appointment and went for a visit.

On my visit with the cardiologist, he took an EKG, Echocardiogram,
and a stress test. He then informed me that I had a weak heart with an
ejection fraction of thirty to thirty five percent. The normal range is fifty
five to seventy percent. I was diagnosed with Viral Cardiomyopathy, a
disease of the heart muscles that makes it harder for the heart to pump
blood to the rest of your body and can lead to heart failure.

"Dr., I am a runner, running is good for the heart, it strengthens it,
my cholesterol levels are great, I have no plaque what happened here?" I
asked. He then began to ask me a bunch of questions to determine how
it might have happened. I know my uncle died of a heart attack, but
other than that I did not know anyone else in my family to suffer with
heart disease. He then looked at my history with having the flu every
year at times twice per year and not having it treated. He said a virus
can damage it and since you were having the flu every year, it looks like
it was caused by it. It can be treated with medications- more so an Ace
inhibitor like lisinopril and a beta blocker like metoprolol to improve
the pumping ability, improve blood flow, and lower the blood pressure.
He prescribed these two meds for me. He told me that I would have
to decrease my stress levels and he advised me not to enter any more
races, to stop running, no more marathons, and to walk instead. Now I
had no choice but to take these meds. I began to take it but within three
months I had to stop taking the lisinopril. It was a great drug for this
disease but I learned it had some very serious side effects. Two of which
I experienced, dry cough and angioedema, swelling of the tongue. I informed him, and he changed it to losartan (cozar). After taking losartan
for two days, I began to experience palpitations, my heart began to race,
and I was feeling so sick. I went to the ER to check it out. In the ER they
took another echocardiogram, this time my EF was forty five%, which

meant that the lisinopril and metoprolol was effective. If only I did not have a side effects to it, it would have been great. Now they had to find another ACE inhibitor or one that would work with the metoprolol to increase my EF and strengthen the heart muscles.

I had just turned fifty and everything was already going south for me. *It is going to be tough for me not to run, how can I quit running again?* I said to myself. First it was my father, now a disease that took away my passion. Running was my peace. It was a bit of an escape for me at times when the going got tough, but I enjoyed it so much, it became my happy place and was part of me. Coping with this disease was not easy, but it was not as difficult as coping without being able to run and enter races. Walking, which is the alternative, does not work for me. I attempted it but soon became bored. I had to find some other form of physical activity that I could do that would relax me, keep me in good shape, and allowed me to maintain a healthy lifestyle. I got a gym membership, began to do weight lifting and body shaping workout exercises, and went to clubs more to keep dancing. This helped me maintain a lower stress level which the cardiologist encouraged. My friend Carlene took it pretty hard when told that I could not run any more like we use to. She lost a running buddy. At times I thought she was still in denial because she would still ask me to come running with her. I often had to remind her, but what I did was accompany her on her run by walking instead. I did this for a while but did not enjoy it. I finally reached the acceptance stage of my grief for running and realized that this was my new reality and if I wanted to live I had to do what was right for me. I would keep the faith, my running days were over but my life continues I told myself.

Chapter 18

My Life Now

It's been two years since my ruptured brain aneurysm. I am healthy, happy, and well contended with who and where I am in my life today. I now live in the sunshine state of Florida and continue to practice nursing at a hospital nearby, so close that I walk to work. It's Saturday, early September, at the end of summer 2018 and as I sit on my balcony, relaxing and watching the clear blue skies and the sun beaming in all its glory, I can't help but to soak up every minute of everything that lies before me. The palm trees that line the sidewalks are swaying from the winds and the cool breeze from the water feels so good on me. I lay back taking in some of the beauty of life that is being displayed in front of me. The boats, the jet skiers, the yachts, are cruising and racing in the waters of the intercostals while men and women line the banks with their fishing hooks fishing as their children play nearby. Runners run on the sidewalks shared by dog walkers while motorcyclists do their tricks on their bikes in the center of the streets while vehicles pass by. I am reminded by each of these things how precious and enjoyable life is or can be, but at the same time it can be gone in a second and how important it is to live in the moment and enjoy the beauty that surrounds me, and I am so grateful that I am still here to soak up all its beauty.

Many people in this world are afraid of changes or terrified to make changes in their life that at times is necessary for growth. We are afraid to close doors that should be closed and allow for new ones to open. Thirty one years ago, I left my parent's nest and closed one chapter of my life in search for a new one and to begin a journey on my own. I had to make many changes, and many were made for me through challenges experienced. Some included changing residency many times, cars, and jobs. Through all these changes I have seen tremendous growth within myself. People who do not know me but learned of my story would often say "You have gone through so much and did so much for others you should quit working, go on disability and enjoy yourself." To those people I ask why quit? I am blessed to have experienced this and come through without any deficit, stronger and better than I have been, plus quitting is not in my DNA. Besides, I am living in the best of two worlds, I am living and enjoying a retirement type lifestyle, engaged in all kind of activities, dancing more, socializing more while working full time. If I had quit I do not believe I might have reached this point of contentment in my life. I still have so much to give and it brings me so much joy caring and giving myself each day to my patients and my brothers and sisters of this world.

The aneurysm was somewhat of a blessing in disguise for me. It has changed me quite a bit. It has brought me from a period of darkness to a light as bright as day. Having seen the light and embraced the light I now feel a tremendous sense of peace, a peace I have not felt before. It has lifted me spiritually to new heights. I have become more spiritual, more engaged in learning the scriptures and how to better serve my God. I now feel I have become closer to my God. I have also noticed I am not as skeptical as I used to be, but more trusting and open. I am seeing life through a new lens. I do not sweat the little things any more. I have become more forgiving of others, a better listener and as a result have more patience with my patients. Having had my aneurysm and hospitalized for a long period of time, I have become a better nurse as I now have both perspectives; one of a nurse and one of a patient. The path is no longer dark but clearer, this light is now guiding my every step. I have accepted my new reality and I am using my platform to encourage and inspire others to keep the faith, to never give up, to live a healthy life style and when blessed always pay it forward, to believe in something other than themselves and stand up and fight for that belief if and when you have to. To continue to hope, for when you hope it gives you something to look forward to and it keeps the energy around you positive.

THE GIFT OF LOVE
AND
THE FINE LINE BETWEEN LOVE AND HATE
By
ROSALIND NOREIGA

L- Love is a tiny four letter word that is lifting, it can bring about peace, but it is filled with mixed emotions. It makes you laugh - it brings about joy, it can make you cry- it brings sadness. According to Maslow we need love for it is one of our basic needs for survival. However it often gets lost.

O- When love is lost it leaves one overwhelmed with grief. If this grief is unresolved or uncontrolled it often leads to hate which easily turns into revenge that may lead to violence, and now that fine line between love and hate is crossed.

V- This special gift called love can be victorious if only we can keep it in our hearts and lives, when it is shared, when we make it contagious, infectious or spread it like wild fire, only then shall we all win.

E - Love although it is meant to be given unconditionally we humans often place expectations on it, as we all want to be loved in return.

TO LOVE IS TO BE KIND
TO LOVE IS TO BE GENTLE
TO LOVE IS TO BE GIVING
TO LOVE IS TO BE FORGIVING
FOR LOVE CONQUERORS ALL

We live in a nation that has lost it love for one another and hate has made its way in. There is now a desperate need to regain that love. THEREFORE- MY PEOPLE LET'S SPREAD THE LOVE FOR IT SHALL BRING PEACE AND ERADICATE THE HATE.

Acknowledgements

Kyle Noreiga, (my son), for his part in the editing of this memoir and for his tremendous support in my recovery.

Dr. Armonda, Dr. Lieu, and Lisa for their part in saving my life and for their unselfish act by taking time off from their busy schedule to conduct an Aneurysm Support group for their patients. Giving their patients an outlet to share their stories, concerns and gain support from each other which have proven to be a great help in the healing process.

To all my friends, too many to name, you know who you are, for your kind, generous support, your prayers, your love during those difficult times and most of all for not giving up on me. Your tremendous support has been a key in my great recovery.

To all the nurses, therapists, and support staff at Washington Hospital Center who cared for me during my hospitalization.

Robert Hicks, my dearest friend for helping me understand the teachings of the Bible and encouraging me to keep the faith.

Printed in the United States
By Bookmasters